Praise for *A Comprehensive RTI Model: Integrating Behavioral and Academic Interventions*

"*A Comprehensive RTI Model* is a 'must read' for every educator. Not only does Shores provide the background information of RTI for academic achievement and behavioral functioning, she also takes the reader step by step to effectively integrate the two processes. Students will benefit from school teams who implement the information."

Ronda Shelvan
Autism Consultant/Special Education Teacher
Washougal School District
Washougal, WA

"This book is a practical guide on how to mesh behavior and academics. It will provide schools that are implementing RTI with clear and practical ideas on how to integrate both behavior and academics into one comprehensive model. The book provides examples, case studies, and resources for both academics and behavior that are very useful for teachers and administrators."

Judy Rockley
State Trainer, Kansas State Department of Education
Olpe, KS

"The information presented in this book flows succinctly and is well written for both RTI novices and experts to understand the important role behavior plays in the RTI process and in overall student achievement. It's an excellent roadmap for building sustainable reform."

Cassandra Allen Holifield
Author, National Presenter, Behavior Specialist, and Special Educator
Director, Northwest Georgia Learning Resources System
Acworth, GA

"I recommend Cara Shores' book to all educators as they strive to raise student achievement in their schools! This is a great resource for school psychologists, teacher educators, teachers, and administrators for developing their RTI structure and supports. This book offers research-based methods and interventions in a user-friendly format. An important aspect of the book is the chapter on laying the foundation and promoting buy-in for comprehensive RTI implementation. Finally we have direction for sustainable reform! The process development tools provided with this book make it a valuable school resource."

Donna Lee
Program Specialist, West Georgia Learning Resources System
Columbus, GA

I believe that every teacher wants to be remembered by at least one student as "the favorite." I dedicate this book to two of my favorites, Mr. and Mrs. Opal Lovett of Jacksonville State University. Mr. Lovett taught me to see the world in a different light while Mrs. Lovett taught me to express what I saw in a way so that others could see it as well. These two wonderful people devoted their lives to countless students from around the world. They are shining examples of what all educators should be.

A COMPREHENSIVE RTI MODEL

Integrating Behavioral and Academic Interventions

CARA SHORES

CORWIN
A SAGE Company

For information:

Corwin
A SAGE Company
2455 Teller Road
Thousand Oaks, California 91320
(800) 233-9936
Fax: (800) 417-2466
www.corwinpress.com

SAGE Ltd.
1 Oliver's Yard
55 City Road
London, EC1Y 1SP
United Kingdom

SAGE India Pvt. Ltd.
B 1/I 1 Mohan Cooperative
    Industrial Area
Mathura Road, New Delhi 110 044
India

SAGE Asia-Pacific Pte. Ltd.
33 Pekin Street #02–01
Far East Square
Singapore 048763

Printed in the United States of America.

Library of Congress Cataloging-in-Publication Data

Shores, Cara.
  A comprehensive RTI model : integrating behavioral and academic interventions / Cara Shores.
    p. cm.
  Includes bibliographical references and index.
  ISBN 978-1-4129-6294-0 (cloth)
  ISBN 978-1-4129-6295-7 (pbk)
  1. Problem children—Education—United States. 2. Learning disabled children—Education—United States. 3. Behavior disorders in children—Treatment—United States. I. Title.

  LC4802.S46 2009
  371.93—dc22

2008052419

09 10 11 12 13 10 9 8 7 6 5 4 3 2 1

Acquisitions Editor: David Chao
Editorial Assistant: Brynn Saito
Production Editor: Appingo Publishing Services
Cover Designer: Scott Van Atta

Contents

About the Author

 **Cara Shores** received a BA in English from Jacksonville State University and MEd and EdS degrees in special education from the University of West Georgia. She taught special education in both pullout and inclusion classrooms at the elementary and middle school levels. Cara has served as a building-level administrator, system SST and 504 coordinator, and director of special education. In 2000 she served as the principal author of the Georgia DOE Student Support Team Resource Manual. She also served as a consultant on several federally funded projects for inclusion. As president of Wesley Educational Services, Cara presents to school personnel across the United States and Canada. She is a feature presenter for the Council for Exceptional Children. She is the author of *Positive Outcomes: Utilizing Student Support Teams as a Tool for School Improvement.* She is coauthor of *Response to Intervention: A Practical Guide for Every Teacher* and *Using RTI for School Improvement: Raising Every Student's Achievement Scores.*

Acknowledgments

Writing a book is never the result of one person's efforts. Many talented people contributed to this work. I would like to express heartfelt gratitude to the following friends, colleagues, and mentors: Kim Chester, Victor Morgan, and Gail Wilkins for encouragement and expertise; and to Lamar Barnes, Wes Dickey, Kristy Arnold, and Linda Hatcher for invaluable assistance in school implementation issues; and special thanks to David Chao, Brynn Saito, Belinda Thresher, Cassandra Holifield, and Donna Lee for patience and expertise. And, as always, love and appreciation to my boys, Scott and Wesley, for sticking with me through another one.

PUBLISHER'S ACKNOWLEDGMENTS

Corwin gratefully acknowledges the following reviewers for their contributions:

Cassandra Allen Holifield
Director, Northwest Georgia Learning Resources System (GLRS)
Northwest Georgia Learning Resources System/RESA
Rome, GA

Donna Lee
Program Specialist
West Georgia Learning Resources System
Columbus, GA

Margaret McLaughlin
University of Maryland
College Park, MD

Tonya Midling
Program Supervisor, Special Education Learning Improvement
Office of Superintendent of Public Instruction
Olympia, WA

Ronda Schelvan
Autism Consultant/Special Education Teacher
Washougal School District
Washougal, WA

Karen Tichy
Associate Superintendent for Instruction
Catholic Education Office, Archdiocese of Saint Louis
St. Louis, MO

A Comprehensive Model for Response to Intervention

Response to Intervention (RTI) is a term that most educators are at least somewhat familiar with by now. Since its inclusion in the Individuals with Disabilities Education Improvement Act of 2004 (IDEA), RTI has been promoted as an effective tool for the identification of students with learning disabilities. Additionally, the RTI process has been integrated into school improvement plans throughout the United States and Canada in efforts to raise achievement of all students. In these instances the process is used for academic purposes, working to improve the reading and math skills of children in Grades K–12.

However, there is another equally effective side to RTI—one that addresses behavioral functioning for all students within the school. Although it has not gained as much attention as the academic process, it is not new. Numerous schools have implemented this approach for more than ten years. Some components of the process were, in fact, included in IDEA in 1997, seven years prior to the academic model, through IDEA's requirements for positive behavioral supports. The behavioral model has been heavily researched and found to be effective in significantly reducing problem behaviors within a school.

It has long been established that academic functioning and behavioral functioning are intertwined and inseparable in classrooms (Scott, 2001; Sugai, Horner, et al., 2000). Effective classroom management serves as an important part of the foundation for successful classroom instruction. Teachers cannot teach unless they can manage their students' behavior. Likewise, some students misbehave because they are trying to avoid an instructional task that they feel they are unable to perform.

It is this complementary relationship between academic performance and behavioral functioning that prompted the writing of this book. The purpose is twofold: (1) to provide background knowledge and guidance to school systems as they seek to implement RTI as a behavioral model, and (2) to integrate the academic RTI process with the behavioral components, giving administrators, teachers, and policymakers a common language and a clear picture of how the two processes may become one.

THE EVOLUTION OF RTI

Response to Intervention involves an instructional framework of increasingly intensive assessment and interventions designed to address a continuum of academic and behavioral problems. The process has more than thirty years of research substantiating its effectiveness. In 1977 Deno and Mirkin studied the impact of providing standard protocol interventions to students at risk for reading failure. Targeted reading interventions were provided to small groups of children based on specific skill deficits. Student data derived from curriculum-based measurement (CBM) was used to measure growth and make additional instructional decisions. This process was found to be very effective in increasing reading achievement (Deno & Mirkin, 1977).

At the same time, Bergan (1977) researched a problem-solving approach to address student behavior and academic problems. In his study a team developed interventions based on individual student needs. These interventions were taught to the student as appropriate and adjusted as needed through ongoing problem-solving meetings. This approach has been used for many years as a method of identifying and addressing student deficits prior to referral for special education evaluation (D. Fuchs, Mock, Morgan, & Young, 2003).

These two distinct processes have merged into the current RTI framework. It is most commonly represented as a three-tiered pyramid, as shown in Figure 1.1. This multi-tiered representation reflects a public health perspective that provides preventive health services for the general population, treatment services for mild to moderate illnesses, and intensive services for severe illnesses (Chafouleas, Riley-Tillman, & Sugai, 2007). Likewise, RTI provides for strong curriculum and instruction for all students within the school, targeted interventions for students who continue to exhibit learning and behavioral problems, and intensive interventions for students with the most significant needs.

Academic Support

As stated earlier, RTI implementation for the purpose of addressing academic problems has received a great deal of attention since 2004.

Figure 1.1   Standard Protocol Model

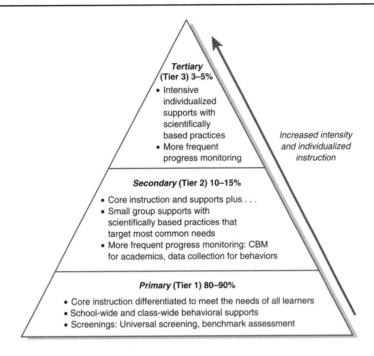

Tertiary
(Tier 3) 3–5%
• Intensive
   individualized
   supports with
   scientifically
   based practices
• More frequent
   progress monitoring

*Increased intensity
and individualized
instruction*

Secondary (Tier 2) 10–15%
• Core instruction and supports plus . . .
• Small group supports with
   scientifically based practices that
   target most common needs
• More frequent progress monitoring: CBM
   for academics, data collection for behaviors

Primary (Tier 1) 80–90%
• Core instruction differentiated to meet the needs of all learners
• School-wide and class-wide behavioral supports
• Screenings: Universal screening, benchmark assessment

President George W. Bush established the Commission on Excellence in Special Education in 2001 for the purpose of studying special education issues and making policy recommendations. Among other issues that were addressed was the long-standing dissatisfaction with the use of the significant discrepancy model for establishing eligibility for specific learning disabilities. In this regard, the Commission made a bold assertion that many children placed into special education without adequate documentation of their responsiveness to scientific, research-based instruction were essentially instructional casualties rather than children with disabilities (President's Commission on Excellence in Special Education, 2002). Other groups, such as the National Summit on Learning Disabilities, the National Research Council Panel on Minority Overrepresentation, and the National Institute for Child Health and Development Studies, reflected the findings of this report in recommendations that RTI be considered as an effective method for identifying students with learning disabilities (Bender & Shores, 2007). The Individuals with Disabilities Education Improvement Act of 2004 (IDEA) contained a provision that allowed states and local school systems to consider a student's response to scientific, research-based intervention when determining the existence of a learning disability (IDEA, 2004). Further, the law prohibited states from mandating the use of only significant discrepancy formulas for determining eligibility. Under the new law, states and local educational agencies could use RTI data as one piece of evidence of a learning disability.

Most states are in the process of incorporating RTI into their special education regulations. According to a survey of all state special education directors published in October 2007, twenty-four states had finalized requirements for mandatory, transitional, or permissive RTI implementation at that time. Twenty-three states were considering implementation, but had not made definite decisions about specifically how the process would be developed (Zirkel & Krohn, 2008). However, the overall focus was on an academic RTI process, based on IDEA recommendations.

There is a large body of research supporting RTI for increasing academic achievement. Both short- and long-term studies have shown dramatic increases in reading (Kamps et al., 2008; Simmons et al., 2008) and math achievement (Bryant, Bryant, Gersten, Scammacca, & Chavez, 2008; L. S. Fuchs et al., 2006) when interventions are delivered through an RTI framework. Similar findings have proven the effectiveness of the model for specific types of learners, such as those learning English as a second language (Vaughn et al., 2006).

That leads us, then, to the question of whether or not RTI can be used as effectively for behavioral interventions as it has been for academic interventions. Is there a strong research base for a multi-tiered behavioral intervention model? Can behavioral interventions be incorporated with academic ones? How is the process similar to and different from one based strictly on academic interventions? We will explore the answers to these questions throughout this book.

Background and Research for Behavioral Support and Interventions

In the 1980s an approach to behavior management called Positive Behavior Interventions and Supports (PBIS) began to emerge. This approach focused on proactive and preventive rather than aversive and punitive behavioral techniques. The principles of applied behavior analysis (ABA) were used for the first time in classroom settings. With ABA, a student's behavior is analyzed to determine how he or she is being influenced by external factors. Rather than having interventions implemented by behavior experts through clinical-type services, PBIS initiated a focus on strategies implemented by teachers and families in the students' natural environments (Turnbull et al., 2002). Interventions were designed not only to decrease problem behaviors, but also to improve the quality of life for students exhibiting those behaviors (Janney & Snell, 2008).

This approach continued to gain momentum as requirements for behavioral assessment and supports were included in the 1997 reauthorization of IDEA. This law required school personnel to conduct functional behavior assessments and develop behavioral support plans for all students with disabilities whose behavior impeded their own learning or the learning of others (U.S. Office of Education, 1999, sec 300.520). In addition, the law specified that children with behavioral difficulties who were being considered for special education eligibility must receive a functional behavioral assessment as part of their eligibility evaluation. These requirements were reiterated in IDEA 2004 and were supported by a provision that federal funding could be used for training teachers, administrators, and other school staff in positive behavioral interventions (Council for Exceptional Children [CEC], 2005).

During the same time frame, efforts were being made through general education initiatives to make schools safer and more manageable. The National Education Goals Panel (2000) set a priority that U.S. schools would be free of drugs, violence, and weapons, and would "offer a disciplined environment conducive to learning." This gave further support to a framework for positive and proactive behavioral management.

In response, the U.S. Department of Education, through the Office of Special Education Programs, established the National Technical Assistance Center on Positive Behavior Interventions and Supports. This center was designed to provide assistance to states, districts, and schools as they develop systems for positive discipline and behavioral management. Through its work with various state and local agencies, the center compiled a multitude of materials and resources for use by schools in developing their own process of positive behavioral supports. By 2007 more than 5,000 schools were implementing School-Wide PBIS through the National Center for Positive Behavior Interventions and Supports (Horner & Sugai, 2007b).

Despite the efforts that have been made to encourage schools to develop positive behavioral management systems, many schools and districts have not responded and still struggle with high incidences of violence and school suspensions. During the 2003–2004 school year, 81 percent of public schools reported one or more violent incidents. Additionally, 27 percent reported daily or weekly student bullying, 11 percent reported verbal abuse of teachers, and 17 percent reported gang activities (Dinkes, Cataldi, Kena, & Baum, 2006)

However, it is estimated that most behavior problems in schools are exhibited by 25 percent or less of the school population. The most significant problems, often resulting in multiple days of school suspension, are carried out by only 3–7 percent of the population (Scott, 2001). Historically, schools have attempted to address these problems through punitive consequences and have placed little emphasis on school-wide behavioral management. However, the statistics outlined above are powerful evidence that this plan has proven ineffective.

Researchers have found a direct relationship between a school's ability to manage overall student behavior and its ability to impact severe behaviors (Scott, 2001; Sugai, Horner, et al., 2000). When expectations for all students' behavior are clearly defined, overtly taught to students, and reinforced throughout settings, minor behavioral problems are reduced, leaving more time and resources for students who need additional supports. Outcomes reported by schools with PBIS processes and by larger statewide initiatives are impressive. The following examples are indicative of positive results from PBIS implementation.

Tigard-Tualatin School District, Oregon
- Office discipline referrals in an elementary school decreased by 35 percent in one school year.
- Office discipline referrals during lunch decreased from 10 percent in the fall of 1998 to 4 percent in the fall of 1999 (Sadler, 2000).

Iowa Behavioral Initiative
- Office discipline referrals in 75 percent of cohort schools (24 schools represented) experienced a 42 percent average decrease per day per 100 students across a two-year period.
- Both instructional and administrative time wasted by behavioral incidences was significantly reduced (Mass-Galloway, Panyan, Smith, & Wessendorf, 2008, p. 132).

Bangor School District, Pennsylvania
- Office discipline referrals were reduced in elementary and middle school by 30–40 percent (Lohrmann-O'Rourke et al., 2000).

In addition, research studies have substantiated increases in the consistency of behavior management procedures among staff members and increases in positive interactions between staff and students. Other studies have shown that implementation fidelity for both academic and behavioral interventions is higher in schools using this framework (Simonsen, Sugai, & Negron, 2008). It is evident from this and other similar data that a tiered intervention model for behavior is not only effective in decreasing behavior problems, but has the potential to significantly increase student achievement by providing more time for instruction and improving the school environment.

Ongoing research supports the idea that the most effective strategy for promoting positive behavior in schools is to focus on expectations and consequences. Proactive approaches in which students are directly taught expectations and rewarded for compliance are proving effective with most students (Baer, Manning, & Shiomi, 2006; Cohen, Kincaid, & Childs, 2007; Sprick, Garrison, & Howard, 1998; Sugai, Sprague, Horner, & Walker, et al., 2000). These concepts form the basis of positive behavioral approaches through Response to Intervention. The RTI process provides a framework for meeting these criteria by offering research-based strategies and systems to help schools raise academic achievement, increase safety, decrease problem behavior, and establish positive school cultures (Kincaid, Childs, Blase, & Wallace, 2007).

This is accomplished through increasingly intensive supports and data-based decision making. Schools develop school-wide management plans, incorporate these plans into the daily workings of the school, and provide a framework for reinforcing compliance. Students in these schools are taught what behaviors are expected and held accountable for meeting expectations. In addition, these schools have measures in place to provide additional supports to students who continue to exhibit behavioral problems.

Integration Into One Comprehensive Model

Recently, more attention has been given to research and recommendations that promote integration of an academic and behavioral model for RTI. Horner and colleagues (Horner, Sugai, Todd, & Lewis-Palmer, 2005) stressed that academic and behavioral supports must be interconnected in order for children to reach their learning potential. In reality it is often impossible to separate academic and behavioral difficulties. In a meta-analysis comparing reading only, behavior only, and comprehensive integrated models, researchers found that students made more significant gains in both reading and behavior through the comprehensive model (Stewart, Benner, Martella, & Marchand-Martella, 2007). Combining these approaches into one comprehensive RTI model provides appropriate supports for students who exhibit deficits in either or both areas.

In many schools it is estimated that hundreds of instructional hours and an equal amount of administrative work hours are lost yearly because of time spent dealing with behavioral problems. As illustrated earlier, implementation of a support structure for behavioral management increases instructional time for teachers and provides more time for administrators to address curricular issues. In the Iowa study discussed previously, researchers sought to estimate administrative and instructional time gained from reductions in office discipline referrals. Based on information gathered from administrators in participating schools, researchers estimated that, for each referral avoided, administrators gained ten minutes and teachers gained twenty minutes of instructional time. This translated to a range of 43 to 239 hours of instructional time and 21 to 119 hours of administrative time per school. It was noted that this finding was key in helping administrators decide whether or not to establish a behavioral RTI model within their schools (Mass-Galloway et al., 2008). The benefit lies in both the reduced number of behavior problems and increased time spent on instruction.

A comprehensive RTI model embraces the tiered framework, addressing both academic and behavioral needs through an increasingly intensive continuum of interventions and progress monitoring. The model illustrated throughout this book will be a three-tiered model, as depicted in Figure 1.1. However, it is important to align a new behavioral framework with an academic RTI structure that may already be in place in the school. Therefore, leadership teams should adapt the example presented in this publication to match the number of tiers in their existing framework. These and other critical implementation issues will be discussed in detail in Chapter 2.

In our model, Tier 1, also called Universal or Primary Supports, involves instruction for all students through general education and universal screening to identify students who need additional instruction. In Tier 2 targeted interventions are put in place for nonresponders. Progress is monitored closely, allowing teachers to adjust interventions based on student response. Tier 2, also called Secondary or Targeted Supports, provides targeted intervention for small groups through general education (L. S. Fuchs & Fuchs, 2007). When these interventions prove to be insufficient, more intensive supports and progress monitoring are provided through Tier 3, also called Tertiary or Intensive Supports.

The behavioral components used in this book, although based on the structure of School-Wide Positive Behavior Interventions and Supports, will encompass more than the typical PBIS model. The purpose for this is to provide usable information to administrators and teachers who work in schools not involved in a state or district PBIS implementation project.

As schools seek to implement a comprehensive RTI model, they must put into place several essential elements critical to the success of the process. These elements are assessment through universal screening and progress monitoring, research-based interventions, data-based decision making, and implementation fidelity. We will explore these elements through an overview of the comprehensive framework. In subsequent chapters we will look at these elements much more closely within each tier.

An important first step in using RTI is to screen all students for academic and behavioral deficiencies. Universal screening involves using a standard measure to compare students to a benchmark (e.g., seventy-five words per minute in oral reading fluency), expectation (e.g., fewer than four office discipline referrals per year), or peer group (student places at 70th percentile in math problem solving). These screening tools are commonly used three or four times per year in order to identify students who need additional support.

The most common universal screening tool for behavioral indicators involves data collection regarding the number of office discipline referrals (ODRs) a student receives during the year (Sandomierski, Kincaid, & Algozinne, 2007). However, as we will see in Chapter 3, additional measures should be used to identify withdrawn students or those who have fewer ODRs but still experience significant behavioral problems. Teachers may also complete behavior rating scales or collect data on specific events that occur, such as the number of times a student yells out in class. Additionally, teachers may identify students with characteristics that place them at risk for behavioral problems. The data obtained through these measures is used to identify which students are not successful with the school-wide management that is in place and therefore need additional supports.

As students move to Tiers 2 and 3, assessment becomes more intensive in its frequency and scope. This is accomplished through progress monitoring. Its purpose is to carefully monitor student response in order to make instructional adjustments. Progress monitoring for academic achievement often involves the use of curriculum-based measurement probes that allow the teacher to compare actual performance with expected performance. For example, oral reading fluency is assessed by determining the number of words read correctly in one minute. The data derived from this assessment helps the teacher determine if the student is on track to reach the expected end-of-year benchmark. If the student performs below expectation, the teacher may adjust instruction either through the current tier of instruction or by allowing the child to receive instruction at a more intensive level at the next tier.

Behavioral progress monitoring often involves closely watching and evaluating the same data that was derived from universal screening, but to a more intense level. In Tier 1 the student may be identified as being at risk because he has three office discipline referrals (ODRs) in a two-month period. The student would receive a more intensive intervention in Tier 2 and the team would monitor his ODRs biweekly to judge his response to the intervention. Progress monitoring may also include data obtained through direct observation of student behavior. For example, a teacher may record the number of times a student is out of his or her seat in a thirty-minute period. This data may be collected as often as daily in order to determine whether the intervention is working to reduce the inappropriate behaviors.

If students are unresponsive to Tier 2 interventions, or in instances where students exhibit extreme behaviors, Tier 3 interventions may be added to those used at Tier 2. A functional behavioral assessment may be performed to determine why the behavior is occurring and to aid teams in developing appropriate interventions and supports.

Data-based decision making is a critical feature in the RTI process. Student data should be collected as often as necessary in order to make sound instructional decisions. Later in this book, specific recommendations for assessment tools and data management will be discussed.

The use of research-based interventions is another critical feature of RTI. These interventions are systematically provided for students based on their level of need. Academically, RTI provides targeted interventions specific to the student's deficit in reading, math, or other content areas. For example, a student with poor reading fluency will receive Tier 2 interventions that specifically target oral reading fluency. Another student may receive interventions that target reading comprehension or math problem solving, based on his or her individual needs.

Behaviorally, the process seeks to change the environmental factors, such as particular occurrences (called antecedent events) that lead up to a misbehavior, and/or to change settings where behavior problems occur (Sandomierski et al., 2007). RTI focuses on prevention by working to reduce both current behavioral problems and long-term, chronic problem behaviors (Barnett et al., 2006). Leadership teams use data-based decision making to analyze data and make instructional and structural decisions regarding student support and interventions.

In an effective RTI model, Tier 1 involves teaching school-wide behavioral expectations to all students. Rewards and consequences are established to support these expectations. Proactive measures are put in place to prevent problem behaviors from occurring (Waguespack, Vaccaro, & Continere, 2006). This system of behavior management should enable teachers to manage minor behavior infractions and increase overall time on task (Barnett et al., 2006). A standardized social skills curriculum may be used to implement this tier. In a well-designed program, it is estimated that 80–90 percent of students will be successful with this level of support alone (B. Walker, Cheney, Stage, & Blum, 2005).

It is imperative that schools have an effective Tier 1 process in which the majority of students experience success prior to identifying at-risk students and developing Tier 2 interventions. In the absence of a quality

Tier 1 process, schools will be overwhelmed with large numbers of students in need of targeted interventions, thus limiting the outcomes for all students.

Tier 2 interventions are provided to individuals or small groups of students who continue to exhibit behavioral problems despite Tier 1 implementation. Approximately 10–15 percent of students will need this level of support (Horner et al., 2005; B. Walker et al., 2005). Interventions for these students should be evidence-based and may include social skills training, school counseling groups, or conflict-resolution skills training (Lane, Wehby, Robertson, & Rogers, 2007; Sandomierski et al., 2007; B. Walker et al., 2005). These interventions are provided in addition to, not instead of, Tier 1 implementation. In order to promote fidelity of implementation, they should be easy to implement and require limited time and resources from the staff.

When students prove unresponsive to Tier 2 interventions, Tier 3 supports may be added. These interventions are individualized to meet the specific needs of the student. A team approach is effective in developing behavioral and academic plans for students at this level. It is estimated that only 3–5 percent of students in a school will require this level of intervention (Horner et al., 2005; B. Walker et al., 2005). However, the amount of time and resources required to support these students is often significant. In some instances this small percentage of students accounts for 40–50 percent of all behavioral problems in many schools (Sugai, Horner, & Gresham, 2002). These students may require intensive academic interventions as well, often needing individualized instruction for large blocks of time in order to make adequate progress.

When comparing academic and behavioral RTI components, many similarities are evident. In both processes RTI implementation must be based on the use of high-quality, research-based interventions and practices provided to all students and targeted individuals as needs are identified. All stakeholders must implement these interventions with fidelity across settings. Student response must be measured through ongoing progress monitoring. Data must be used to adjust instruction and interventions as needed. As student deficits become more intense, so too must the interventions and progress monitoring. In addition, data obtained through observation and other forms of documentation is used to measure implementation fidelity of the curriculum and targeted interventions. The differences between the two models lie in the actual tools and interventions used in each. Otherwise, strong correlations exist.

FORMATS FOR IMPLEMENTATION: STANDARD PROTOCOL AND PROBLEM SOLVING

Response to Intervention may be carried out through various formats, namely the Standard Protocol and Problem-Solving Models. Both of these formats follow the tiered RTI framework, in which students progress through the tiers based on their response or nonresponse to interventions provided. The main difference between the two is the way determinations are made in regard to interventions, service delivery, and progress monitoring.

Standard Protocol is more commonly used to address academic deficits. In this approach classroom teachers provide a research-validated, quality curriculum to all students within the general education classroom (Tier 1). They use universal screening or benchmark assessment to identify students within the group who are at risk for failure. These students are then placed into small instructional groups (Tier 2), in which they receive an explicit, research-based intervention that has been preselected to address the most common student deficits. These groups (usually comprised of three to five students) have been prearranged and are available to all struggling students at the first sign of difficulty. Each student's progress is monitored through curriculum-based measurement. Students who achieve the benchmark through this supplemental instruction return to Tier 1. Students who do not make adequate progress may eventually progress to Tier 3, which provides individualized instruction to students, possibly through special education. Progress monitoring tools are again used to document student achievement.

Standard Protocol may also be used in certain instances for behavioral interventions. For example, students with behavioral problems may participate in small-group, preestablished interventions such as anger management, conflict resolution, or grief counseling. Counselors, social workers, or school psychologists often lead these groups. Students are identified as needing these interventions based on universal screening measures such as number of ODRs or teacher observation, comparing their behaviors with those exhibited by their peers. They may also be identified by teachers, parents, or students themselves as experiencing significant crises or stressors. For example, students may participate in grief counseling to address internalizing or externalizing behaviors following their parents' divorce or death of a significant person in their lives. Student progress may be monitored by carefully following the original data that identified the student as being at risk.

Again, Standard Protocol is distinguished from Problem-Solving in that all components—intervention, grouping, progress-monitoring tools,

Figure 1.2   Standard Protocol Flowchart

intervention time frame, and so on—are prearranged based on the most common needs of students within the school. All students proceed through the tiers in a similar manner with the data guiding the decision-making process. Figure 1.2 provides an illustration of the typical Standard Protocol format. There are numerous examples of this format within the current RTI literature (D. Fuchs & Fuchs, 2005; L. S. Fuchs & Fuchs, 2007; for a thorough discussion of this format, see Shores & Chester, 2008).

By contrast, the Problem-Solving Model involves individual planning for students throughout each tier. A Problem-Solving team determines each student's individual needs and develops an intervention plan designed specifically for that student. This format is commonly used in behavioral interventions. For that reason, the remainder of this chapter will take a step-by-step look at this format as it applies to the comprehensive RTI model, specifically for addressing behavioral problems.

The Problem-Solving format, as stated earlier, involves a team approach. This team should include the student's teachers and other professionals who have knowledge about the student and/or expertise in behavioral planning. This may include a school psychologist, school counselor, administrator, special education teacher, or behavior specialist. The student's parents should always be included. There may be other significant individuals, such as mentors, relatives with whom the student has a strong relationship, or others from outside the school setting who would also serve as valuable members of the team. In general, the further the student moves up the pyramid, the more individuals with specialization and expertise should be included on the team.

The team utilizes a problem-solving cycle that helps team members understand the student's behavioral problems and design strategies that specifically target the causes of the problem. This process is applied in every tier of the pyramid. Figure 1.3 illustrates the cycle.

Step 1: Define the Problem

The team begins by defining the behavioral problems exhibited by the student. The behavior should be described specifically and in measurable terms. For example, "Johnny gets out of his seat an average of nine times in a thirty-minute class period" is measurable and very specific about Johnny's behavioral problem. In contrast, "Johnny can't sit still" is too general and cannot be measured. Teachers should be objective in describing the problem and refrain from making broad generalizations or judgment statements.

The team should discuss the student's response to the school-wide and/or class-wide behavioral plan, describing how the student's behavior is different from his peers and how he or she responded to any interventions and consequences that might have been imposed. It is important to note any patterns that are associated with the misbehavior, such as setting (e.g., unstructured or loosely structured events and environments) or peer group influences (e.g., misbehaviors most often occur when certain students are around). All relevant data regarding behavior frequency and intensity should be carefully analyzed and discussed. The Brief Behavioral Assessment Tool found in Resource C can be used for this purpose.

Figure 1.3   Problem-Solving RTI Model

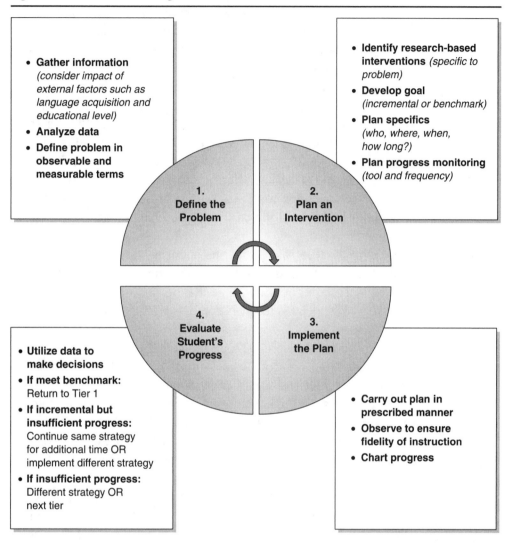

During this step, teams should also consider external factors that are contributing to the student's behavior. The purpose of this is not to make excuses for why the student cannot meet expectations, but instead to determine the level of support needed. Students living in dysfunctional home situations, experiencing loss or turmoil in their families or communities, or living with other significant stressors will be impacted by these events. These events are often triggers for behaviors carried out at school. Students experiencing these stressors may need intensive intervention. This level of intervention may include a process known as Wraparound, which involves a focus on family and community as well as school issues (see Chapter 5). It is also important to be aware of these external factors when conducting intensive assessments, as we will see in Chapter 5.

Working with students with behavioral problems in a classroom setting often causes adults to lose patience, perhaps more so than when working with academic issues. It is sometimes easy for adults, in their frustration with the situation, to lose sight of the fact that the student's behavior may be the result of external factors or significant unmet needs. It is important to separate the child from the behavior. In other words, a child should know that adults care for him, even though they may not like his behavior at the time. If this assurance is not evident, efforts to change the behavior may be more difficult than necessary. Statements such as "He is mean," "He is uncontrollable," or "He doesn't belong in my classroom" only lead to damaged rapport with the student and the parents and prohibit effective behavior management.

The same can be said about the tendency to make judgment statements about students. I recently read a mother's account of her son's experiences in school. She stated that her son struggled throughout elementary school. His teachers complained that he was unable to sit still or remain quiet at appropriate times, couldn't keep his hands to himself, and always wanted to be the center of attention. During his fifth-grade year, her son was diagnosed with attention deficit hyperactivity Disorder and began taking Ritalin. He took the medication for two years with minimal positive results. One teacher's statement stood out in this mother's mind. The teacher said to her, "Your son will never be able to focus on anything" (Winerip, 2008, p. 4).

That young man's name was Michael Phelps, winner of fourteen Olympic gold medals in the 2004 and 2008 Olympic games. The U.S. national swim team coach Mark Schubert had this to say about Phelps's pursuit of his eight gold medals in the 2008 games: "I think you have to be realistic as to how incredible this effort is. It has to do with his physical ability, his ability to race, his ability to focus, to get excited when he needs to get excited, to get down when he needs to get down" (Michaelis, 2008, p. 2A). In other words, Michael could focus on something. In fact, some of the very things that got Michael into trouble in school helped him become the most famous swimmer in history. The teacher who said he would never *focus* on anything made a judgment statement based on her opinion and perception of the current situation. Although Michael may have struggled in some areas, it was unfair and inappropriate to generalize that to all areas. Wouldn't it have been wonderful to be the teacher who saw Michael's potential and encouraged him to pursue big things? Luckily, Michael's mother and his swim coach saw it. Teachers must always keep in mind that their words and actions often have a lasting effect on a student's life. Comments made out of frustration may do more harm than is ever realized.

If the student's behavior problems have existed for only a brief time, the team should carefully consider whether they might actually be caused by these external factors. If the student has a long history of these behaviors, the team should consider how the factors might be contributing to the behaviors themselves or to the student's response to previous interventions. For example, students who live in an apartment complex where violence is common may be more likely to exhibit violent behaviors themselves. The student may need intensive interventions designed to teach him or her alternative methods for handling anger or stress.

Finally, the team must examine the student's academic functioning. It is estimated that as many as 80 percent of students with behavioral problems also have academic deficits (Scott, 2001). Many times, students exhibit behavioral problems in an effort to avoid or escape difficult tasks (Waguespack et al., 2006). As was already discussed, many researchers and practitioners assert that behavior and achievement are inseparable and should never be considered in isolation (McIntosh, Chard, Boland, & Horner, 2006). Therefore, as the team examines a student's behavior problems, it is advisable to also review benchmark assessment or universal screening data to determine academic functioning levels. If the student is found to have academic deficits, interventions for those deficit areas should be implemented concurrently.

Some students in the RTI process will require more extensive assessment during this process. Students who are unresponsive to Tier 2 interventions should be given a Functional Behavioral Assessment (FBA) in order to identify why the student is engaging in inappropriate behaviors (Waguespack et al., 2006). FBA involves a process of systematic data and information collection about a student's behavior and the antecedents and consequences surrounding it (Gresham, 2003). FBA is instrumental in planning interventions for all students with behavioral problems and may be used with children who are unresponsive to Tier 1 universal interventions. It is most commonly used with Tier 2 nonresponders. It is required for students with emotional behavioral disorders and is sometimes an integral part of evaluation for other areas of special education eligibility.

In addition to FBA, student information and data may also be obtained from teacher and parent questionnaires and checklists (Ellingson, Miltenberger, Stricker, Galensky, & Garlinghouse, 2000). Like FBA, this is most often used for students who are unresponsive to Tier 2, but can be helpful in planning for all students. In addition, direct observations are very effective in providing anecdotal information as well as specific data. As a general rule, as behaviors become more intense, so do the evaluation methods. These methods will be discussed in more detail in subsequent chapters.

Step 2: Plan an Intervention

After defining the problem, the team must develop a behavioral plan using a proactive intervention designed to keep the behavior from occurring and, in some cases, teach a replacement behavior. The intervention should be one that is easy for the teacher to implement and provides an appropriate amount of supervision and support for the student.

The chosen intervention should also be supported by research. Both No Child Left Behind and IDEA define research-based practices and interventions as

> research that involves the application of rigorous, systematic, and objective procedures to obtain reliable and valid knowledge relevant to education activities and programs and includes research that
>
> - employs systematic, empirical methods that draw on observation or experiment;
> - involves rigorous data analyses that are adequate to test the stated hypotheses and justify the general conclusions drawn;
> - relies on measurements or observational methods that provide reliable and valid data across evaluators and observers, across multiple measurements and observations, and across studies by the same or different investigators;
> - is evaluated using experimental or quasi-experimental designs in which individuals, entities, programs, or activities are assigned to different conditions and with appropriate controls to evaluate the effects of the condition of interest, with a preference for random-assignment experiments, or other designs to the extent that those designs contain within-condition or across-condition controls;
> - ensures that experimental studies are presented in sufficient detail and clarity to allow for replication or, at a minimum, offer the opportunity to build systematically on their findings; and

- has been accepted by a peer-reviewed journal or approved by a panel of independent experts through a comparably rigorous, objective, and scientific review. (NCLB, 2001)

However, the term as defined here specifically applies to processes addressing academic deficits. IDEA applies the requirement that interventions have a research base when evaluating RTI for use in identification of learning disabilities. On a broader scale, NCLB requires that all programs operating within a school have a research base. Despite the fact that there is no direct reference in either law that specifically requires a research base for behavioral interventions, it is generally accepted throughout the educational community and considered best practice that all interventions have a research base. The purpose is to ensure, to the maximum extent possible, that strategies and interventions are likely to produce positive results.

When applying the concept of research-based interventions to those addressing behavior, there is one significant difference. That difference lies in the type of evidence used to support the intervention. The Center on Positive Behavioral Interventions and Supports divides evidence-based practices into three categories. The first group consists of interventions with scientific evidence that meets NCLB requirements. This includes interventions that have been researched through single-subject design. Next, the center identifies practices based on program evaluation, analyzing implementation and outcome, but without the controls necessary to meet NCLB standards. Finally, the center identifies a group of evidence-based practices derived through case studies involving one or a small number of students. The second and third groups, although not usually considered sufficient for academic interventions, provide valuable information for the appropriateness of behavioral strategies (Barnett et al., 2006; National Technical Assistance Center on Positive Behavioral Interventions and Supports, 2007). This is especially true when the interventions are clearly explained through implementation manuals that are scripted or very explicit in their instructions and application (Carter & Horner, 2007). As a general rule, teachers should use caution when choosing behavioral interventions from the second and third groups. The center recommends pilot implementation until additional data can be collected (National Technical Assistance Center on Positive Behavioral Interventions and Supports, 2007).

The team may also identify a replacement behavior that will be taught concurrently. A replacement behavior is one that is more appropriate than the undesirable behavior and generates an outcome that is similar to that achieved by the original behavior or satisfies the student's need for attention, approval, or other purposes. For example, a student may be taught to raise his hand rather than yelling out answers in class. When he receives positive feedback for raising his hand, he receives the attention and approval that he initially desired.

Next, the team must establish a goal for the student. This may involve deciding if any incidence of the behavior is acceptable. For example, one or two incidences of yelling out in class in a thirty-minute period would probably be acceptable and manageable through the classroom management plan. Twelve incidences in the same time period would indicate a need for additional support and interventions. The team might set a goal for this student that allowed no more than two incidences in thirty minutes. The behavior would not be completely extinguished, but would be considered manageable once the student reached that goal.

When working toward this final goal, students should be rewarded for meeting incremental goals along the way. For example, an interim goal for this student would be to reduce occurrences of yelling out from twelve times to ten times. When he reached that goal, he would receive a reward. A new goal of eight times would then be set. This would continue until the benchmark or ultimate goal was reached. It is important to remember that, for many students, long-term goals seem unreachable. These students may have a difficult time maintaining focus to work for a reward that is two weeks away. Interim goals in which the student is rewarded more frequently must be used if any progress is to be made.

After the team has chosen an intervention, a replacement behavior if appropriate, and established a goal, they must spell out the specifics for implementation. The following questions should be answered as needed for each student:

- Where will the intervention be implemented (e.g., all classes, special area classes, reading class)?
- What type of data will be collected to substantiate whether the student meets his or her goal?
- How will the data be collected and recorded?
- How often will data be collected?
- Who will be responsible for collecting data or overseeing the student's response (e.g., teacher, paraprofessional, student)?
- How often will data be reviewed?
- What type of reward will be given?
- Will interim goals be established?
- How will the replacement behavior be taught?
- How will the replacement behavior be rewarded?

- Will part of the plan be carried out in the home (e.g., rewards, intervention)?
- How will the teachers communicate with the parents?

Step 3: Implement the Plan

After the team has developed a thorough plan containing all appropriate elements outlined above, the next step is to implement the plan with fidelity. There should be some type of documentation, whether through third-party observation or teacher self-evaluation, that the intervention was implemented as designed. This serves as documentation that the student has received appropriate instruction and management routines, ruling out lack of instruction in behavioral aspects and the student's lack of understanding of behavioral expectations as the cause of misbehavior. Ensuring fidelity of instruction is a critical component in every tier of the pyramid. This concept will be expanded upon in future chapters.

It is always helpful to chart the student's data, providing a visual representation of progress. This allows the team to easily interpret the data and look for additional patterns that may be affecting the student's behavior. For example, some students have increased behavioral problems following weekends or school vacations. This is easily observed when the data is in chart form. Behavior charts are most helpful when paired with anecdotal information regarding antecedents, settings, and consequences. Teams can then compare highs and lows in the data with specific events documented in the anecdotal records. Data may be charted by an adult who is conducting observations or implementing interventions, or it may be charted by the student through self-management.

Step 4: Evaluate the Student's Progress

The final step in the Problem-Solving cycle occurs as teams evaluate data in order to make adjustments in instructional programming. In academic RTI models, Tier 2 interventions are left in place for ten to twelve weeks or more in order to document nonresponse as evidence of a possible learning disability (Shores & Chester, 2008). When addressing behavioral problems, however, it is important to review the data often to make adjustments as necessary. Data review meetings should be held approximately every two weeks. This will allow teachers, parents, and the student to see progress and adjust the plan if needed. If after two weeks the student is meeting incremental goals, the team should continue with the plan. However, if no incremental goals have been met, the team must determine (1) if the intervention is appropriate, (2) if the student needs further adjustments to the environment, and (3) if the student needs more intensive interventions.

After an appropriate amount of time with an intervention, the team must make instructional decisions regarding appropriate next steps. The student may remain in Tier 2 with the same intervention, return to Tier 1 if the benchmark goal has been met, or move to Tier 3 if the team decides more intensive interventions are needed. With behavioral interventions there seems to be no standard definition for "appropriate amount of time" in the research literature. However, teams should always remember that behavior change often occurs in very small steps. They must take that into account as they make decisions regarding acceptable progress. Decisions should always be based on student response data. When interventions are unsuccessful, changes should be made to the intervention itself or to the intensity of implementation.

Throughout the Problem-Solving process, teams should frequently consider all factors that may be impacting the student's performance. Data should be carefully examined to determine appropriateness of interventions and the need for an instructional change. Teams should continually strive to address both academic and behavioral needs of learners through this structured process.

BARRIERS TO COMPREHENSIVE RTI IMPLEMENTATION

As with any school improvement initiative, RTI is not without certain barriers to its implementation. Many teachers are limited in their knowledge of research-based interventions for both academic and behavioral issues. Progress monitoring is not widely used above the elementary grades, perhaps due to the limited number of standardized tools available for older students. Many districts have limited financial resources and, therefore, are hesitant about committing those resources to comprehensive schoolwide efforts. Educators may also experience difficulty seeing behavioral and academic approaches as one comprehensive RTI model. In current RTI literature and research, terminology is different for academic approaches than for behavioral approaches. For example, the tiers in an academic framework are sometimes termed as core, strategic, and intensive. Those same tiers in a behavioral framework may be termed primary, secondary, or tertiary (Sugai, 2008). This can become quite confusing for those seeking to understand and develop their own district plan.

In addition, there are some barriers that are specifically related to behavioral components of the model. One of the most significant problems is the fact that many educators see appropriate behavior as something within the child rather than a skill to be taught (Eber & Hawken,

2008). Many teachers believe that their job is to teach students academic skills and content knowledge, but feel they are not responsible for teaching students to behave appropriately. Traditionally, behavior management was taught at home by parents. However, that cannot be assumed in today's society. Because of societal changes, twenty-first century schools have a variety of service providers that were not considered necessary even thirty years ago. Examples of this include school nurses, counselors in elementary schools, social workers, and law enforcement officers. Society has changed, and schools have had to change with it. We cannot assume that children are taught behavioral skills at home. If educators want students to meet certain behavioral expectations, they must explicitly teach those expectations and support students as they learn.

A second barrier involves the quality of implementation. When school faculty members fail to carry out behavioral plans effectively and consistently in Tiers 1, 2, or 3, the overall program quality is compromised (Eber & Hawken, 2008; Kincaid et al., 2007). When this occurs and students fail to respond to Tier 1 or 2 interventions, it is impossible to rule out lack of instruction or appropriate supports as the cause for the misbehavior. Unfortunately, lack of consistency in behavior management is considered to be common among both new and veteran teachers (Kincaid et al., 2007; Sprick et al., 1998).

Additionally, behavior management is often viewed as the responsibility of individual teachers. In many schools there is no school-wide behavior plan in place. This lack of a universal system in Tier 1 requires teachers and administrators to spend time dealing with mild behaviors on an individual basis. An effective school-wide plan provides consistent expectations, rewards, and consequences that often prove sufficient for approximately 80–90 percent of the students, thus significantly reducing time spent on mild behaviors (Horner et al., 2005; B. Walker et al., 2005). Research shows that teachers use a limited repertoire of behavior interventions, often using the same strategies and consequences when dealing with students exhibiting mild and moderate behavior problems. These strategies may be too severe for some students, but not strong enough for others. When early intervention is not provided in a timely manner and with sufficient intensity for students with severe behaviors, problems often escalate quickly and end up costing more in resources, time, and potential impact of later interventions (Eber & Hawken, 2008).

Finally, with both academic and behavior interventions, schools often fail to use data for instructional decision making. Instead, decisions are based on perceived effect and anecdotal information. This has been one of the major criticisms of the Problem-Solving RTI model overall (D. Fuchs et al., 2003). In order for RTI to maintain integrity in regard to quality of interventions and student responsiveness, decisions must be driven by both individual and systemic student data (Kincaid et al., 2007).

If schools are to effectively develop and implement a comprehensive RTI model, each of these factors should be given careful consideration and attention. Building-level administrators play an especially important role in leading teachers to embrace the vision of the process. Whether the school is undertaking this process under the umbrella of a state plan or venturing in through their own initiative, implementation should always be preceded by a well-developed plan addressing all aspects of the school program. It is crucial to consider issues such as school climate and readiness for a behavioral management program, staff development requirements, leadership team structure and membership, and integration with a possible existing academic process. If RTI is completely new to the school, it is even more important to address these issues.

SUMMARY

Response to Intervention is a well-researched process proven to increase achievement and reduce behavior problems when implemented effectively. The academic and behavioral models have many commonalities and are more efficient and effective when implemented as one integrated comprehensive model. The Problem-Solving process provides the structure and support necessary for behavioral planning. Implementation of a well-designed RTI model can serve as the framework for an effective school improvement model.

The remainder of this book will explore the comprehensive RTI model in detail. Chapter 2 will discuss ways to lay the foundation for an effective process by developing a vision and promoting buy-in. Chapter 3 will explore the essential components of Tier 1. The remaining chapters will discuss the critical elements of Tiers 2 and 3. As you progress through the book, I encourage you to apply the examples and recommendations to the systems already established in your own district or school. When integrated with programs already in place, RTI can serve as a next step in a long-range plan for overall school improvement.

Establishing the Structure for RTI Implementation

Over the past few decades, public schools have experienced a multitude of reform efforts, many of which have been necessitated by societal changes. As student populations have changed to include large numbers of children who have special challenges or learning needs, such as English Language Learners, those living in poverty, or children experiencing the effects of homelessness, teachers have had to adjust their teaching practices to address a wide variety of abilities and learning styles. It is no longer acceptable to "teach to the middle" and hope most students learn.

The same is true for behavior management and discipline. It is no longer acceptable to rely on punitive measures alone in managing student behavior. As discussed in the previous chapter, traditional behavior management techniques have been unsuccessful in creating safe learning environments. Schools continue to report large numbers of violent incidences including bullying, verbal abuse of teachers, and gang activity (Dinkes et al., 2006). At the same time, pressure has been placed on schools to keep students in class. Rather than removing students through in-school or out-of-school suspension, educators are urged to develop processes that will manage behavior within the school and classroom setting.

However, lasting change in policy and practice is sometimes difficult to achieve in schools. Teachers are often skeptical of new programs and hold to the idea that each one will pass in due time. Educators express concern that the rapid changes in student population, legal accountability, and basic pedagogy experienced in schools since the mid 1990s have made teaching more difficult than at any time in the past. As an educational consultant teaching about inclusive practices and RTI, I have been told by veteran teachers that they will bide their time until the trend has passed. In the meantime they will continue to use the strategies that they have held to, often not considering that these strategies might be less effective than newer methods.

In facing these obstacles, educational leaders may ask themselves if it is indeed possible to bring about sustainable school change. The answer, fortunately, is a resounding "Yes!" There are numerous examples of schools across the United States that have experienced significant reform efforts and produced lasting positive results. In their book *Whatever It Takes*, DuFour and colleagues (DuFour, DuFour, Eaker, & Karhanek, 2004) highlighted four U.S. schools that had undergone extensive reform efforts. The process in each school involved the development of professional learning communities in which the staff worked as one unit to raise expectations for all children. The transformations took place over a number of years and required that the faculties embrace the vision that all students would learn in their schools. It involved the implementation of numerous strategies including frequent monitoring of student progress, extended learning time for students at risk, and a pyramid of interventions that provided a continuum of increasingly intensive levels of support. In other words, these schools used the essential components of RTI to transform their schools.

In order to determine the factors that promote sustainable reform, L. S. Fuchs and Fuchs (2001) examined schools where reform efforts had been successful and schools where they had been unsuccessful. They outlined their findings in a list of principles necessary for sustainable reform. These principles provide guidance for schools as they develop school improvement plans. Let us examine each of them in order to set the stage for our discussion of leadership and district plan development.

The first principle highlights the importance of having a key individual lead the reform process. Significant reform efforts have stemmed from the vision of one person. Whether at the state, district, or school level, a dynamic leader is able to share her vision and bring others along with her. Later in this chapter, the principal's role as key leader in the school will be highlighted. However, the principal may not be the originator of the idea within the district. Neither does it have to be a central office administrator. There are numerous examples of one teacher whose passion for raising student achievement inspires and transforms an entire school or district. It is this passion that encourages others to follow into new ideas and methods.

The second guiding principle involves control of resources. L. S. Fuchs and Fuchs (2001) found that schools must have some discretionary control over personnel and financial resources. As school districts develop system plans, they should work toward consistency between schools, but also allow flexibility based on individual school needs. For example, schools will vary in their choices for reward systems based on the interests of their students. They should have flexible funding options for providing these rewards. Along those same lines, schools may use existing personnel for different purposes. While it is true that schools must always follow state and federal funding and use guidelines, districts may permit some flexibility while still meeting these guidelines.

Next, it is important to build accountability for student outcomes into any plan (L. S. Fuchs & Fuchs, 2001). As schools seek to adopt school-wide management plans and individual student interventions, they should keep a constant focus on raising student outcomes. Data should drive the decision-making process. When it becomes evident that students are not making acceptable progress, the staff must work together to find more successful methods and interventions. The leadership team or total faculty should continually examine student data and current practices to determine where changes need to occur. In highly effective schools, every staff member takes responsibility for the achievement of every student. I find it frustrating when I am told that a school would have made Adequate Yearly Progress had it not been for the performance of a particular sub-group. That statement often speaks volumes about how well the staff works together. If any students in the school are unsuccessful, regardless of whether or not they have a label, it is the responsibility of every staff member to work together to find solutions for those students.

When that type of collegiality is accomplished, it lays the foundation for the next principle, which is tolerance for initial implementation difficulties (L. S. Fuchs & Fuchs, 2001). Problems will occur with any new process. Initial stages may bring unforeseen circumstances, unexpected student responses, and less than desirable initial data. Therefore, it is important for all those involved in implementation to make a commitment to work through those problems. As difficulties occur teachers and administrators must rely on this commitment and seek alternatives. It is important to remember that no lasting change occurs without some initial difficulties. There is a significant difference between adjusting a program as needed based on data and abandoning the program at the first sign of difficulty.

Lastly, it is important to recognize and celebrate accomplishments (L. S. Fuchs & Fuchs, 2001). This is true not only for students, but also for the faculty and school as well. So often teachers are blamed for problems when they occur, but never thanked for their successes. Districts should celebrate school achievements on a regular basis. Likewise, schools should celebrate individual teachers and students who excel in their efforts. Recognition should come from a variety of places, including parents, community, and the media. Although monetary rewards would be wonderful, most recognition comes through intangible means. For example, an

Atlanta news program employs a reporter who is responsible for recognizing the accomplishments of schools, teachers, and students. This thirty- to ninety-second spot on the morning news is an excellent source of commendation and pride for school districts across the entire northern part of Georgia. This is a refreshing change from the critical press that schools so often receive.

These five principles of successful reform efforts may surprise some and seem trivial to others. They don't involve large sums of money or vast numbers of new personnel. Instead, they involve leaders who work to develop a successful plan to guide the process and a staff who is willing to take on the challenge of teaching ALL students. Table 2.1 provides reflective questions related to each of these principles. As you read through these questions, consider how the principles apply in your school or district.

Table 2.1   Reflective Questions About Your Implementation of Essential Components for Sustainable Reform

1. Recognize the importance of a key individual.
   - Is there an individual or team who is leading the RTI implementation process in your district or school?
   - How is the vision of RTI's potential for school improvement being shared?
2. Give schools flexible control of resources.
   - How will schools be given discretionary control over resources and faculty?
   - Will principals and leadership teams be allowed to choose interventions and rewards based on their students' needs and preferences?
   - Will they have flexibility in determining roles and responsibilities of staff members in order to provide interventions?
   - How will they be held accountable for their choices?
3. Create accountability for student outcomes.
   - How often will individual, class, and school data be reviewed?
   - Who will assist schools in reviewing this data?
   - Who will assist schools in providing guidance for using data for school improvement?
4. Have tolerance for initial implementation difficulties.
   - Is there an understanding among all involved that RTI implementation takes time and is not without barriers?
   - Is there a commitment to persevere despite these barriers?
   - How will schools be supported as they overcome barriers?
5. Recognize accomplishments.
   - How will schools, staff members, and students be recognized for their accomplishments?
   - How often will this take place?

SOURCE: Adapted from Fuchs, L. S., & Fuchs, D. (2001). Principles for sustaining research-based practice in the schools: A case study. *Focus on Exceptional Children, 33*(6), 1–14.

Implementing school improvement efforts is a challenging task. With any new initiative, there is a period of learning and questioning the value and overall benefit of the change. Many times school improvement efforts are begun with little time and attention given to developing vision and buy-in from administrators, teachers, parents, and students. Requirements and rules are put in place with no real explanation as to their benefit, and no time is spent establishing acceptance from those who will be implementing the program. In such instances the efforts may prove to be unsuccessful.

RTI can only be effective in schools where there is a commitment shared by all that every student can be successful, both academically and behaviorally. For many schools this will involve moving away from a mind-set where punishment has been the only system for dealing with inappropriate behavior. This involves a change in the overall school culture and belief system that may be deeply rooted in the current climate (DuFour et al., 2004). Without this change of mind-set, lasting reform will not occur.

Change of this nature does not occur overnight. Most researchers agree that RTI implementation requires a multiyear implementation process (OSEP Center on Positive Behavioral Interventions and Supports, 2004; Taylor-Greene & Kartub, 2000). I recommend that schools and districts plan for a three- to five-year implementation period. Time must be allocated for program development, training, and implementation in logical steps. Districts and schools should work to develop an explicit and comprehensive long-range plan. This plan should be based on current strengths and weaknesses as well as projections for future expansion and growth. Several excellent resources designed to assist districts in this process are listed in Table 2.2.

The focus of this chapter is the development of a framework and structure for implementing a comprehensive RTI model through the development of behavioral components. This behavioral framework can be added to an existing academic framework or developed as a new entity. Each step in district- and school-level implementation will be described in detail. A summary checklist outlining the process is available in Resource A. Throughout the chapter, much attention will be given to process assessment, in which districts and schools evaluate their need, readiness, and openness for the model. There is a great deal of foundational work to be done before problem-solving meetings are held and interventions are begun. Taking time to build this foundation will increase the likelihood of creating a successful and sustainable program.

Table 2.2   Resources for Comprehensive RTI Plan Development

- Council of Administrators of Special Education
  Response to Intervention: Blueprints for Implementation
  www.casecec.org
- Positive Behavior Interventions and Supports
  www.pbis.org
- RTI Action Network
  www.rtinetwork.org
- National Center for Learning Disabilities
  www.ncld.org
- Response to Intervention Tools
  www.rtitools.com
- Learning First Alliance
  www.learningfirst.org
- National Center on Response to Intervention
  www.rti4success.org
- RTI Summit
  www.rtisummit.org/resources_fedprj.asp
- IDEA Partnership Project
  www.ideapartnership.org/page.cfm?pageid=28
- Teaching LD (click LD Resources, then Current Practice Alerts)
  www.teachingld.org
- Shared Work.org
  www.sharedwork.org
- National Association of State Directors of Special Education
  www.nasdse.org
- National Center for Research on Learning Disabilities
  www.nrcld.org
- Technical Assistance Center on Social Emotional Learning for Young Children
  www.challengingbehavior.org
- Center for Early Literacy Learning
  www.earlyliteracylearning.org

DISTRICT-LEVEL IMPLEMENTATION

As previously discussed, one critical factor for reform sustainability is the guidance of strong leadership beginning at the state or regional level (Sindelar, Shearer, Yendol-Hoppey, & Liebert, 2006). Many state departments of education have developed School-Wide Positive Behavior Interventions and Supports projects that provide ongoing support and training. These programs are often highly developed with numerous resources available to school districts that choose to participate. Programs in Maryland, Florida, Illinois, and Ohio are just a few of the exemplary projects operating throughout the United States. However, as mentioned earlier, this is not true in all states. In a 2006 survey of all fifty states, it was found that forty reported having materials relevant to PBIS implementation. When these materials were compared with PBIS recommendations, only ten states addressed all twenty-five components considered necessary for implementation (Killu, Weber, Derby, & Barretto, 2006).

Even in states without PBIS projects, there are individual school districts that have done an excellent job with the process. When district-level leaders commit to the principles of RTI, they can build a support system for their individual schools that can be highly successful. This should be a combined effort of all areas of leadership, including curriculum, instruction, assessment, student support, special services, finance, and human resources. There should be a mind-set of joint ownership in which all departments work together to develop an appropriate structure for the district (Hilton, 2007). Often, two or more individuals from the areas of curriculum, assessment, instruction, and/or special education work together to facilitate and lead RTI implementation. This small group will be responsible for the preparatory work involved in putting together an implementation plan. They should be knowledgeable about the RTI process and how it fits into the existing school improvement plan. They may work for a considerable period of time developing a vision for RTI in the district prior to beginning full implementation.

I recommend that district planning begin with the establishment of a leadership team. Teams of this type are helpful in providing guidance through initial and ongoing stages of implementation. In addition, they help with teacher and parent buy-in by giving each group a voice in the decision-making process. The leadership team should be representative of all key stakeholders including district and building administrators, teachers, support personnel, community members, and parents. This team will be responsible for evaluating current practices and needs, developing a long-range action plan, and providing ongoing evaluation of the RTI process. Table 2.3 presents a list of responsibilities that are often assigned to this team.

A first step in forming this team will be to provide members with a thorough understanding of the RTI process and why it is needed within the district. The facilitators should spend as much time as necessary presenting and discussing achievement and behavioral data for the district and individual schools. They should provide an overview of existing programs and, with the use of data, identify gaps in the overall plan. Resource A contains a simple Gap Analysis Form that can be used for this purpose. The facilitators should provide an in-depth explanation of how RTI will address identified deficit areas. Their job is to bring this newly formed

Table 2.3   District Leadership Team Responsibilities

- Attend planning meetings.
- Serve as leaders for RTI implementation.
- Develop protocols, guidelines, and procedures for district implementation.
- Analyze district and school data.
- Complete needs assessment.
- Develop multiyear action plan.
- Facilitate and support school-level implementation.
- Complete various checklists for ongoing process assessment.
- Develop in-service training priorities.

team to a consensus and strong belief that RTI will be effective in addressing the identified problems. Leadership team members must ultimately develop a strong vision for RTI implementation within the district and individual schools. In order to do that, each member must believe in the process and embrace that vision personally and professionally.

I have found that one of the best ways to promote buy-in is to show the process in action. There are many examples of schools that have had great success with RTI in both academics and behavior. In Chapter 1 several schools' behavioral results were highlighted. Video examples of successful schools are also very effective in showing how the process can work. An excellent set of demonstration videos is available at www.pbis .org in the video clips link. Many of the examples were produced by the University of North Carolina at Charlotte and illustrate both behavioral and academic RTI processes in schools of the Charlotte/Mecklenburg School District. The clips are well made and feature discussions by school personnel about their own experiences with tiered intervention systems and the tools they use to implement the process.

After reviewing examples of successful programs, the leadership team should discuss similarities and differences between those examples and their own schools. They should discuss how the effective components can be incorporated into their schools and identify additional considerations unique to their situations. In these early steps of team development, it is important not to spend time dwelling on specifics such as which progress monitoring tool or research-based strategy to implement. Instead, teams should work to develop an overall understanding and belief that RTI will effectively and successfully provide a framework for increasing student achievement and decreasing problem behaviors.

It may be helpful for all or some of the district leadership team members to attend one or more regional, state, and/or national conferences on RTI. There are many available from government agencies such as the National Center on Response to Intervention, support agencies such as the Council for Exceptional Children, and private organizations. These conferences can provide team members with a strong foundational knowledge and opportunities to network with other educators at various stages of implementation. In addition, they may provide team members with opportunities to ask questions of RTI experts, researchers, and policymakers in order to resolve their own concerns.

Additionally, or perhaps alternatively, districts may bring in a knowledgeable consultant to work individually with the leadership team. This may be more cost-effective for districts, particularly in situations where the leadership team is made up of a large number of members. The consultant should be willing, when requested, to plan specifically for the district, taking into account system data and existing programs. I strongly recommend that every central office and building administrator attend this initial training. It provides for consistency and reduces confusion in later planning stages.

It is important to provide this level of training for the leadership team early in the process. Once the team has been trained, plans can be made for later staff development for all school personnel. Districts are sometimes tempted to bring in a consultant to work with all teachers in the district before providing this level of training and support to the leadership team. I find that whole school faculties are often overwhelmed by an RTI workshop if they have no foundational knowledge of the concept. The process goes much more smoothly when leadership teams are trained, vision and buy-in are established at the schools, and then staff development is provided for the faculty at large.

Once the leadership team has been trained and a consensus for implementation has been formed, they should begin the process of action plan development. In preparation for this task, teams may choose to complete needs assessment tools and readiness inventories to evaluate current trends and the need for change. One such needs assessment is provided in Resource A of this book. This assessment is designed to assist teams in reviewing current student data in both academics and behavior and identifying priorities for overall plan development. It should be completed by the leadership team early in the RTI implementation process.

In addition, a number of inventories have been developed specifically for RTI behavior implementation. The National Technical Assistance Center on Positive Behavioral Interventions and Supports (NTACPBIS) has many such tools available on their Web site (www.pbis.org). These tools have been designed for School-Wide PBIS implementation and can be adapted to fit the needs of individual districts and schools as they implement RTI. Additionally, many state PBIS sites have different tools or adapted versions of the PBIS tools. Table 2.4 contains a brief description of several tools, recommendations for their use, and information on where they may be obtained. Leadership teams may examine the descriptions and choose the tools that best fit the needs of their district and/or school. Each assessment tool and checklist may need to be modified slightly. For example, the PBIS guidelines require that ten schools in the district be involved in implementation. This may not be appropriate as individual districts seek to implement a comprehensive RTI model. Likewise, some checklists have been developed for accountability purposes for schoolwide PBIS project schools. All components will not be applicable to comprehensive RTI implementation. Despite this fact, the tools are very useful in assisting teams as they develop district and school plans.

Teams may want to begin by completing the Leadership Team Self-Assessment and Planning Tool referenced in Table 2.4. This tool will assist the team initially by helping them determine whether all essential components of the leadership team are in place. It will also give guidance in the beginning stages of developing an action plan. In addition, the Effective Behavior Support Team Implementation Checklist will help teams determine the steps necessary for ongoing RTI implementation.

Another helpful tool is the District Readiness Checklist, also referenced in Table 2.4 (Florida PBIS). This tool provides a summary of the essential components necessary for district implementation and measurable objectives that allow the district to assess its current level of readiness. The checklist was designed for School-Wide Positive Behavior Interventions and Supports and is applicable to overall RTI implementation. It is suggested that the items on this checklist be reviewed yearly to evaluate progress and update action plans (George & Kincaid, 2008).

Teams should carefully examine their current programs for the purpose of identifying gaps in services and determining how existing programs will fit into the RTI process. This will enable the team to see the "big picture" of RTI in the district. For example, many districts have one or more schools that have been involved in the Reading First Initiative. These schools already have many elements of RTI in place, particularly progress monitoring and targeted interventions. A comprehensive RTI model is a natural next step for them. Team members may also identify areas that are not efficiently addressed by existing programs and determine how RTI can fill that deficit. This process will eliminate redundancy and allow for a more seamless approach to school improvement (Crone, Horner, & Hawken, 2004). Table 2.5 provides an example of a portion of

Table 2.4   Tools for RTI Process Assessment

Tool Title	Location	Description
District Readiness Checklist	http://flpbs.fmhi.usf.edu/ProceduresTools.asp	Assesses readiness for change and SWPBS implementation
Training Readiness Checklist	http://flpbs.fmhi.usf.edu/ProceduresTools.asp	Assesses training needs
Benchmarks of Quality	www.pbis.org	Alternative to SET, does not require consultant observations
School-Wide Evaluation Tool	www.pbis.org	Assesses implementation; requires consultant observations
Effective Behavior Support Survey	www.pbis.org	Initial and annual assessment of PBIS in school
Team Implementation Checklist	www.pbismaryland.org	Guides activities of leadership team
Coaches' Checklist	www.pbismaryland.org	Used by facilitators to monitor progress of PBIS implementation
Implementation Phases Inventory	www.pbismaryland.org	Assesses level of implementation
Leadership Team Self-Assessment and Planning Tool	www.pbis.org	Guides team in developing action plans

a gap analysis for an elementary school. The gap analysis form, as mentioned previously, is available in Resource A. Note that the example in Table 2.5 is completed only for a portion of the school's reading services. This was done for the sake of brevity. A school should complete a gap analysis for all areas of instruction and behavior management.

Along those same lines, teams should examine their own district policies to identify any that may conflict or counter behavioral RTI efforts. For example, teams should look carefully at system behavioral policies, including those pertaining to in-school and out-of-school suspension and expulsion. Policies for tribunal procedures should be examined to ensure consistency between old and new requirements and to identify areas that need to be revised.

Table 2.5 Gap Analysis for Elementary School Reading

Area of Need	Program or Process That Addresses That Need	Targeted Population	Effectiveness of Program	GAP-Deficits Still Present That Could Be Addressed Through RTI	Goal
Core reading instruction	Houghton Mifflin Reading in general education classroom	All students	81% of students school-wide meet or exceed standards	19% of students are not meeting standards	100% of students meet standards
Targeted reading interventions	Title 1 classroom instruction	Title 1 eligible students	8% of students served, 62% meet standards	11% of students who did not meet standards do not qualify for services; 38% of students served did not meet standards	Strengthen Title 1 instruction so that 100% of students meet standards
Intensive reading interventions	Special education pullout and inclusion	Special education eligible students	48% of eligible students meet or exceed standards	52% of students did not meet standards in reading; no supplemental intensive reading instruction is offered	100% of students meet standards

It may also be beneficial for the leadership team to complete a cost/benefit analysis (Mass-Galloway et al., 2008). This will give administrators and teachers a clear picture of how much instructional and administrative time can be saved by implementing a strong behavioral RTI framework. This analysis is performed by comparing the number of office discipline referrals with and without the model and the time spent on each referral. Normally, this is done after the first year of implementation using pre- and post-data. However, teams may use this as a preassessment by setting a goal for post-implementation office referrals. A simple cost/benefit analysis tool is available at www.pbismaryland.org/costbenefits.xls.

Districts should identify a funding source for the RTI process. Funding sources vary widely in districts across the United States. The Individuals with Disabilities Education Act of 2004 (IDEA) allows districts to use 15 percent of federal funds to provide early intervening services to students not yet eligible for special education services. Many districts are using these funds to provide training, materials, and staff for RTI implementation. Expenditures may include hiring a district RTI coordinator, but these responsibilities are often taken over by existing personnel. Staff development may represent the largest area of expenditure. As stated earlier, training may be conducted by outside consultants or by existing personnel. Districts may also need additional funding in order to provide behavioral curriculum materials for instruction in all tiers. Many state departments of education have developed an overall standards curriculum, and materials are often present in school counseling or Safe and Drug Free Schools programs. Schools will also need access to incentives and rewards for their students. However, these may be largely funded through business partnerships, donations, or fund-raisers.

The team will need to determine how many schools will participate in initial implementation. In many districts efforts have begun on a small scale involving a few pilot schools. This allows the district to develop an effective process with a manageable number of students (George & Kincaid, 2008). Pilot schools can be very helpful in situations where limited support and resources are available for the district. When the pilot schools are established, the district may "scale-up" its practices, making minor adjustments as needed for individual schools. Districts may want to begin with schools already implementing an effective academic RTI framework and add the behavioral component as the next step. Some larger districts have chosen to begin with one high school, along with the middle and elementary schools that feed into it.

One additional consideration, relating back to our principle of accountability, is to establish a commitment from each school that they will implement the behavioral plans with fidelity. In most projects using School-Wide Positive Behavior Interventions and Supports, each school must have a commitment from at least 80 percent of the staff in order to begin project participation (Sugai & Horner, 2002). This places additional emphasis on vision and buy-in, which will be discussed at length later in this chapter. Because of the nature of a school-wide behavioral RTI process, lack of commitment can undermine the overall success of the program. Inconsistent application of rules and rewards will significantly reduce their effectiveness. Districts should carefully consider how they will work toward this level of commitment in each school. In addition, leadership teams should begin to explore how they will monitor fidelity of implementation in each school.

In developing their system plan, the Eugene School District in Oregon created a list of requirements that each school needed to meet in order to be involved in their project. These requirements were considered to be essential in order for the RTI process to be effective and implemented with fidelity. Schools that were willing to commit to these basic requirements were then given a small financial incentive ($2,000), staff development, release time, technical assistance, and professional development credit for participating faculty members. The requirements were

a. school-wide behavior support as one of its top three school improvement goals for the year;
b. a representative team, including active administrator participation;
c. attendance at three to four team-based training events; and
d. collection of data on the impact of the effort. (Nersesian, Todd, Lehmann, & Watson, 2000, pp. 244–245)

A plan of this type goes a long way toward providing explicit expectations for participation while showing school faculties that they are valued and their hard work is appreciated. With a small amount of advance preparation, professional development plans can be written to give credit toward certification renewal. The financial incentive in this example would provide flexible funding for student rewards. Release time for teachers and administrators to plan or to visit existing successful programs could also be easily arranged. These small steps are highly effective in demonstrating district support for school efforts.

As the district leadership team works through the steps outlined above, they will begin to form their district action plan. This plan should accurately and concisely convey to all administrators, faculty members, parents, students, and community members the sequential steps to be taken in process implementation, along with resources designated to support it. It is very important that the plan show why the process is needed (through data), how it will be implemented, how schools will be supported, and how it will address student deficits. It should show to all involved that RTI can and will serve as the framework to tie together all school improvement initiatives, maximizing the potential for student success.

The time frame for district-level planning for initial implementation should ideally cover six to twelve months. This will allow team members to fully explore all issues and develop a sound plan. However, actual planning time varies greatly between districts. I have seen districts move successfully through this first phase in as little as six weeks. Regardless of the amount of time allowed, teams should explore all the issues outlined above and others specific to their situations in order to put together a thorough implementation plan. I recommend that districts develop both a first-year plan and a long-range, multiyear plan. An example of a multiyear plan is contained in Resource A.

This planning phase represents only the initial work to be done by the district team. Each year the system plan should be reviewed, analyzed, and updated to reflect ongoing student needs. The updated plan should establish new goals and identify resources necessary to support schools in achieving these goals.

SCHOOL-LEVEL IMPLEMENTATION

Once a district plan is in place, it is time for planning to begin at the school level. As mentioned previously, a key characteristic common to schools with successful and sustainable reform efforts, regardless of the level of state and district support, is strong leadership from the building administration. Research consistently demonstrates that the building principal has the most control over buy-in, acceptance, and fidelity of implementation for new programs (L. S. Fuchs & Fuchs, 2001; Gorton, Alston, & Snowden, 2007; Hilton, 2007; Klingner, Arguelles, Hughes, & Vaughn, 2001; Kovaleski, 2007). During a recent study of innovation in schools, Demeter observed the following: "Building principals are key figures in the innovation process. Where they are both aware of and sympathetic to an innovation, it tends to prosper. Where they are ignorant of its existence, or apathetic, if not hostile, it tends to remain outside the bloodstream of the school" (as cited in Gorton et al., 2007, p. 179).

When teachers see active support from their leadership, they are more likely to value the initiative. Building administrators play a vital role in establishing a vision and culture for reform, especially during the initial stages. They should be knowledgeable about RTI and present a positive attitude to the teaching staff. They must also develop their own beliefs about the effectiveness of RTI and resolve any questions they may have. It is difficult for a principal to lead his staff if he still has questions as to the effectiveness of the process.

However, it is also difficult for even the most committed principals to put RTI in place alone. Just as leadership teams play a vital role at the district level, they are equally important at the building level because they give teachers a voice in planning and decision making. As schools begin the RTI process, school leadership teams should be formed in order to take the foundation of the district plan and apply it at the school level (Horner & Sugai, 2000). These team members will serve as a communication bridge between the general faculty and the building and district administration and will go a long way in developing buy-in of the program. Membership should include those who were on the district team as well as other leaders from within the school. Each department should be represented.

School implementation, in many ways, follows the same general process as that used at the district level. The leadership team should develop an action plan specific to their students. In doing so, the group should discuss how their school currently responds when students are not successful. The team may examine current school behavioral and achievement data and identify gaps and weakness areas.

Leadership teams should examine school-wide and class-wide behavioral policies already in place to determine which components are effective and would complement new procedures. For example, current reward systems and recognition programs, such as those for perfect attendance, may be incorporated into the RTI Tier 1 components. Along that same line, some schools already have a problem-solving team whose purpose is to address students' behavioral problems prior to referral to special education. The RTI process can be viewed as an outward extension of this team, providing early intervention for all students.

Ultimately, the team should develop a thorough action plan outlining sequential, manageable steps that will support school-level implementation. This plan should mirror the district plan, but provide additional information specifically related to the needs of the school's faculty and students.

DEVELOPING A SCHOOL CULTURE THAT IS RECEPTIVE TO CHANGE

Just as the district team took time to develop vision and buy-in, so must the school team. Leadership teams must work to develop their vision of RTI into a common vision embraced by the full staff. This vision should be a clear and focused goal that is agreed upon and accepted by the school faculty and serves as the basis for future decisions and planning. Again, teachers must work through their own concerns. They must understand how the process will benefit their students and see that they will be supported in their efforts.

Establishing a vision within a school is sometimes a difficult task. It requires that the leadership present their mission, purpose, and goals in a way that encourages others to embrace them as well. It cannot be forced. Instead, it must be accepted and incorporated into the overall beliefs of the group and the majority of the individual group members. Change is most likely to occur when the new process fits into each teacher's beliefs and teaching style (Hilton, 2007). When group members accept the vision, they develop their own commitment to making the process successful.

Ultimately, all staff members must be committed to implementing the school-wide, class-wide, and individual behavioral plans with fidelity and consistency (Colvin & Fernandez, 2000). Therefore, it is important to spend time assessing and developing a climate and culture that is compatible with the RTI framework. Teams may again use a needs assessment or school climate/culture inventory to initiate the discussion of school change (see Table 2.4). If a process is not accepted within the culture of the school, it will not be sustainable (Waguespack et al., 2006). The leadership team should present data to the full faculty and lead discussion on how RTI will address weaknesses. Again, it is important to establish RTI as an extension of already established programs, with the potential to greatly improve current results.

One factor that encourages teacher acceptance of an initiative is the degree to which it helps struggling students (Hilton, 2007). Long-term acceptance is stronger when teachers are able to see positive student results early in the process (Kovaleski, 2007; Witt & Elliott, 1985). As Tier 1 development is begun, the leadership team should communicate student data to the staff on a regular basis. They should highlight and celebrate even small accomplishments and encourage teachers to keep their own data regarding student behavior in their classroom. This will serve a secondary purpose as a measure of fidelity within individual classrooms.

USING DATA TO DEVELOP AND GUIDE THE RTI PROCESS

It should be evident by now that data analysis is a primary task throughout RTI plan development. It will continue to play a vital role in all phases of implementation, including ongoing program evaluation and individual student planning. Data-based decision making is the driving force in all aspects of the process. As schools develop their framework, they must take into account both outcome and process data. Outcome data reflect student functioning, including responsiveness to interventions. Process data reveal the school and program functioning, including effectiveness of the overall RTI framework. School leadership teams must analyze both process and outcome data in developing a strong action plan.

Teams should first look at school-wide baseline data such as information about office discipline referrals. In doing so, teams may discover settings, time frames, or locations within the school that generate more referrals. These trends are most effectively addressed by altering the setting, placing more supervision in various locations, or changing parts of the school schedule. For example, data may reveal that a particular

> Outcome data give information about student performance. Prior to interventions, Kyle left his seat an average of ten times in a thirty-minute class period. After interventions, Kyle leaves his seat no more than once in the same time period.
>
> Process data depict how well the RTI process is working within the school or district. Central Middle School documented 978 office discipline referrals during the 2006–2007 school year. A comprehensive RTI process was initiated during the 2007–2008 school year. Office discipline referrals for that time frame dropped to 365.

hallway is the site of a large number of incidents. The most logical solution might be to increase supervision in the hallway or limit the number of students in the area at any given time. These types of issues should be addressed in the overall school management plan, which will be discussed in detail in Chapter 3.

Additionally, teams may determine the percentage of students who need interventions in each tier by identifying the number of referrals experienced by individual students. For example, Sugai and colleagues, (2000) suggest that schools consider students with 0 to 1 office discipline referral (ODR) as being successful with Tier 1 supports. Students with 2 to 5 ODRs may need Tier 2 supports and those with 6 or more probably need Tier 3 interventions. Dividing students into these categories will reveal not only how many students need various types of support, but will also indicate the effectiveness of supports in each tier. As stated earlier, approximately 80 percent of students should be successful with Tier 1 alone. Smaller numbers in this category should indicate to the team that Tier 1 curriculum and supports might need to be strengthened.

As they work through this process, teams should analyze their data to determine the effectiveness of current school-wide and class-wide interventions. Teams may look at specific components of the data, such as types of office referrals, grade, gender, and time of year. This type of data analysis will also help identify staff development needs and teachers who need assistance in classroom management. In addition, some teachers may need help in determining which behaviors should be handled in the classroom and which warrant office referrals (Sadler, 2000).

Teams should meet often to analyze and discuss data trends and areas of need. This may be a responsibility assigned to the leadership team or schools may elect to form a data team specifically for this purpose. I often recommend that a separate data team be formed in order to avoid team member burnout. Different types of data should be displayed for students and/or faculty in order to promote behavioral goals and inform about progress. Data illustrating reductions in discipline referrals, number of rewards earned, and overall student achievement are very appropriate for sharing with students. Whenever possible, students should be shown how academic achievement and behavior are correlated. Figure 2.1 shows a sample chart created by one school showing how average grades earned by students were impacted by absences. Students could clearly see from the chart that the average grade dropped steadily with every two days of absence. This made such a powerful statement that one student called 911 when he missed the school bus!

In addition, schools must develop processes for measuring fidelity of RTI implementation, not only for individual teachers, but also for the entire school. The School-Wide Evaluation Tool (SET) is a widely used validated instrument designed to measure implementation fidelity of School-wide Positive Behavior Interventions and Supports. The observer must be trained in instrument implementation, and therefore this instrument may be of limited use to schools not involved in established PBIS projects (Cohen et al., 2007).

An alternate assessment tool that schools may use for self-assessment is the Benchmarks of Quality. It has been found to be reliable, valid, and efficient for use in measuring the effectiveness of Tier 1 implementation. It has several advantages over the SET. Evaluators can be trained quickly through Web training, CD, or in person. It is also quickly administered, requiring approximately ten minutes from teachers and sixty to ninety minutes from the evaluator. Finally, it was found to be consistent across

Figure 2.1 Relationship Between Absences and Average Grade Earned by All Students Within the School

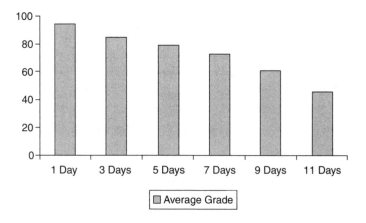

states, regardless of the specific PBIS model in place. Therefore, it may be very appropriate for individual schools and districts seeking to evaluate their RTI behavioral framework (Cohen et al., 2007).

These and other process assessment tools are available on the OSEP PBIS site and/or various state PBIS sites. Their descriptions and locations are outlined in Table 2.4. Regardless of the tool used, teams should engage in ongoing evaluation and assessment of the quality of their program. Evaluation of implementation fidelity should always be a priority. As schools carry out multiyear plans, they should seek to continually improve the quality of their overall RTI process.

Faculty members should have data available to them at all times. In many schools a conference room is set aside to serve as a data room. This room may contain poster-sized printouts of academic and behavioral data. As meetings are held there, student achievement and behavioral data are continually available during both formal and informal faculty discussions.

Because data analysis is so important to the RTI process, leadership teams should secure effective data management systems in order to make information readily available to teams in a variety of formats. Teams should be able to organize data in order to make structural and instructional decisions about school-wide, class-wide, and individual student needs.

It is important for teams to have technology that will support this type of data management. Districts and schools may need to search for software that will facilitate the organization of RTI data. Effective software will allow information to be entered quickly and efficiently and accessed easily through multiple types of reports (Chafouleas et al., 2007).

There are many such tools on the market. For example, EdPlan™, developed by Public Consulting Group, provides a number of data management features including centralized data storage and a variety of charts and graphs. Wisdom Principle has developed a similar program that manages student data and has the added benefit of providing behavioral and curriculum-based measurement tools to be used with RTI processes. Both integrate academic and behavioral components into one data management system.

Perhaps the most widely used program for behavioral data management is School-Wide Information System (SWIS™) developed by the University of Oregon. This Web-based software system organizes and summarizes office discipline referral data for individual schools, but does not manage academic data. SWIS can be used for internal decision making as schools analyze student data, supporting intervention plan design, reporting information to outside agencies, and comparing data across schools (School-Wide Information System [SWIS], 2008).

These are just a few of the products that are commercially available. These tools can make the data management process efficient and easily managed. However, they are certainly not mandatory. Schools may use existing tools such as Microsoft Excel™ to create reports, charts, and graphs.

Both process and outcome data should drive instructional decisions in both academic and behavioral areas. Teachers should be taught to use school-wide, class-wide, and individual data on a daily basis to alter instruction for the purpose of maximizing student achievement and behavioral functioning. Data must be readily available to staff members as they work through the RTI process. During initial development and implementation, the leadership team should use the data available to develop a comprehensive, sequential action plan. As with the district plan, the school team may develop both a multiyear plan and a short-term plan. This will enable the team to prioritize activities while developing an overall vision for RTI implementation.

It is important to understand that process assessment—examining and identifying system strengths, weaknesses, and areas of need—is not a one-time task relegated to RTI development. Process assessment must continue throughout implementation for as long as the framework is in place. Leadership teams at the district and school level should continually evaluate their progress through quarterly and biannual reviews (OSEP Center on Positive Behavioral Interventions and Supports, 2004). They should review process data each year to develop a new action plan that moves the schools forward in their efforts to raise student achievement. Staff development should be considered an ongoing process, both for new and veteran teachers and administrators. The team should also not assume that, once they develop vision and buy-in, they may leave that process behind. This too is a continual process of leading teachers and administrators to accept and embrace the RTI concept.

PROVIDING EFFECTIVE STAFF DEVELOPMENT

A major component of both the district and school actions plans will involve the provision of appropriate professional development for all staff. In any school improvement effort, a thorough staff development program based on the individual needs of the district and school faculties is imperative. Research has found a direct correlation between the learning curve of the students and the learning curve of the faculty and staff (Barth, 2001). In high achieving schools, the adults are constantly seeking to improve their knowledge and skills for working with students.

The staff development requirements for both academic and behavioral components of RTI implementation vary from school to school, but are often quite extensive. From the behavioral standpoint, most general education teachers have received only minimal training in classroom management and individual behavior supports. They will need a thorough understanding of why students misbehave and how some students receive reinforcement from negative consequences. In addition, teachers must learn how their own reactions affect student behavior.

As stated earlier, teachers often become frustrated with student misbehavior much more quickly than with student academic problems. Behavioral problems often create an emotional response from teachers. Many times, in the midst of dealing with a student with chronic behavioral problems, it is easy to lose objectivity. It is also easy to inadvertently add to the student's behavioral problems by responding inconsistently, subjectively, and emotionally. Therefore, teachers must receive assistance in understanding the impact of setting events, negative reinforcement, and functions of behavior prior to dealing with these issues in the classroom. They will need training in a variety of strategies that are effective and easy to implement (Kincaid et al., 2007).

Teachers and administrators will also need training in behavioral data collection and interpretation. Although most collection methods are simple and straightforward, they often differ significantly from what is currently being used in the classroom. For example, placing students' names on the board for misbehavior has long been a common practice in classrooms. However, this is not an effective or appropriate practice for data collection. It often creates a situation in which the student feels like a victim, thereby producing more behavioral problems.

Additional topics for staff development may include training in the problem-solving process, clarifying classroom expectations, establishing an effective classroom management plan, using consequences appropriately, and implementing management plans with consistency. Teachers should also have a clear understanding of the correlation between academic and behavioral difficulties. In addition, teachers may need training in what constitutes an appropriate office referral in order to promote consistency throughout the school.

Staff development needs will vary significantly between schools, even within the same district. While some needs are common to most teachers and can be provided district-wide, others are specific to schools or particular groups of educators such as new teachers or paraprofessionals.

As discussed earlier, schools may initially seek the assistance of an outside consultant or agency to provide either a process overview or in-depth training as part of their staff development plan. However, ongoing support will require expertise within the school or district. It is essential that districts appoint or hire someone to coordinate RTI efforts. This is often a behavioral support specialist, school psychologist, or student services director. This individual is available to provide ongoing support and may have additional assistance from persons within or outside the district. In addition, it is important for all leadership team members to be well trained in the RTI process. This will ensure that the team is able to monitor fidelity of implementation and make informed decisions about program development.

Professional development for all staff may include conferences, workshops, book studies, printed or online support materials, and on-site technical assistance. It is generally agreed that one of these options alone is not sufficient for providing the level of understanding required to have an effective RTI process. A combination of approaches that allows time for teachers and administrators to apply what they have learned and have ongoing discussion and support is the most effective staff development process and will provide the greatest long-term impact (Kratochwill, Volpiansky, Clements, & Ball, 2007).

Another issue that must be considered is that various staff members will need different levels of expertise in behavior management and interventions. All teachers and support staff should be trained in school-wide and class-wide supports. However, as we will see in later chapters, some individuals will need specialized training in assessment and supports for students in Tiers 2 and 3 (Waguespack et al., 2006). Students in these tiers will have problem-solving teams working on their intervention plans on an ongoing basis. Each team will have at least one member with more intensive training in order to guide students' behavioral plans. These individuals may include special education teachers and school counselors. However, it is important to include general education teachers in this group as well. This prevents the perception that intervention tiers are functions of special education.

A variety of resources are available for schools and districts to use in their staff development efforts. One excellent resource is a set of modules developed by Florida's Positive Behavior Support Project. They are available for download from http://flpbs.fmhi.usf.edu under the Resources tab. Topics for school-wide implementation include building faculty involvement, definitions of problem behaviors, and teaching appropriate behavior. Additionally, there are four modules for individual implementation. These modules may save administrators a great deal of time and effort when providing core training for school staffs.

It is important to remember that staff development needs will change from year to year, but will never cease. Schools with successful models report that they must make a yearly commitment to the process and provide ongoing training and support (Colvin & Fernandez, 2000). This will include initial training for new teachers and extension and follow-up for returning faculty members. As the needs of the students change, so must the training for teachers, administrators, and support staff. It is essential that the leadership team continually assess needs and develop a multiyear plan for implementation and support.

INTEGRATION WITH AN ACADEMIC RTI FRAMEWORK

Throughout this chapter the focus has been on development of behavioral components of a Response to Intervention model. The purpose was to clearly define the decisions that are necessary to implement a school-wide behavioral intervention system. However, as I stated at the outset of the discussion, this framework is most effective when implemented with academic components in a comprehensive RTI model.

The comprehensive model is still in its infancy in most schools throughout the United States and Canada. Stewart and colleagues found that, even in schools where both models exist, they are typically isolated from each other in their structure and actual implementation (Stewart et al., 2007). Although there has been much discussion and graphic representations of integrated models, they are seldom implemented that way in schools (Eber & Hawken, 2008).

Horner and colleagues outlined the necessity for an integrated model in their observation that "children will not learn to read by being taught social skills, but they also will not learn to read if a good curriculum is delivered in a classroom that is disruptive and disorganized" (Horner et al., 2005, p. 382). Indeed, behavior and academic success are inseparable. Therefore, this integrated, comprehensive model has the highest probability of increasing overall student achievement (Colvin & Fernandez, 2000; Waguespack et al., 2006).

Each RTI framework is based on the essential elements of research-based interventions, universal screening and progress monitoring, and fidelity of implementation (Shores & Chester, 2008). Each has, as its central focus, universal interventions for all students, identification through assessment of students who need additional supports, and a continuum of increasingly intensive interventions and progress monitoring to meet a variety of student needs (McIntosh et al., 2006).

Perhaps one of the most significant barriers to an integrated model involves the differences in language and terminology used between frameworks. These differences, at first glance, seem to portray two completely different processes. However, the purpose and underlying meaning are essentially the same.

This is evident in even the most basic terms. For example, the academic framework is most often referred to as Response to Intervention while the behavioral framework is commonly called Positive Behavior Interventions and Supports. Likewise, Tier 1 may be labeled universal supports, primary supports, or general education instruction. Yet, regardless of whether the topic is academic or behavioral support, Tier 1 involves core instruction available to all students. The instruction may be in reading skills or behavioral expectations, but both are provided for all students.

Variances in terminology can be attributed to development of the academic and behavioral frameworks by different people at different times. Each evolved with its own characteristics, but both were grounded in a philosophy of early intervention and supports provided on a continuum of increasing intensity. Both depend on universal screening measures for identifying students at risk, targeted research-based interventions, progress monitoring, and data-based decision making.

If schools are to successfully implement a comprehensive RTI model, they must use a common language in order to remove the separation that exists between the two frameworks. While differences may continue to exist in the professional literature, districts and schools should work to minimize these differences and develop a consistent and cohesive language that applies to both sides of the model. It should be clear how assessment, interventions, and procedures are similar or different between academics and behavior. Table 2.6 provides a side-by-side comparison of elements of the comprehensive model in order to demonstrate these similarities and differences.

Most districts and schools will implement a comprehensive model by adding one framework to another that has already been established. This may be quite beneficial in that one framework represents a smaller amount of new knowledge and practices attempted. For example, teachers can learn about and become comfortable with curriculum-based measurement before attempting behavioral assessment. As discussed previously, leadership teams should introduce new components as extensions of already existing programs. The addition of behavioral assessment and interventions to an existing academic framework should be viewed as a next step for increasing student achievement. As districts and schools develop long-range action plans, they should consider how the two frameworks can be merged. The final result will be a comprehensive structure that promotes high levels of student engagement and achievement.

Table 2.6   Comparison of Academic and Behavioral Models

RTI Component	Academic	Behavioral
Universal screening	Summative or formative academic assessment tool	Office discipline referrals, checklists, teacher referral, and others
Research-based interventions	Specific to identified deficit area; should meet NCLB and IDEA requirements	Specific to identified deficit area; may include interventions researched through single-subject design and case study
Progress monitoring	Tiers 2 and 3; curriculum-based measurement	Tiers 2 and 3; interval recording of problem and replacement behavior, assessment of quality of life indicators, and others
Implementation fidelity	Observations of strategy instruction, teacher self-assessment, lesson plan checks	Observations of strategy instruction, teacher self-assessment, checklist completion

SUMMARY

Throughout this chapter RTI has been presented as a school improvement process that requires extensive planning and preparation. This process requires a great deal of foundational work. As administrators seek to set the stage for RTI implementation, there are a number of steps they can take to foster acceptance from their staffs and ensure quality implementation, summarized as follows.

Step 1: Become educated about the process and how it will best fit into the school. Leadership teams, administrators, teachers, and support staff should have a thorough understanding of the RTI process and should be able to apply the process to their current school programs (Hilton, 2007). Implementing an RTI framework should never be approached as a new program. Instead, it should be presented as a "next step" in school improvement processes that are currently underway (Mass-Galloway et al., 2008). This will lessen the tendency for teachers to take a "wait-and-see" approach when deciding whether to accept the practice.

Step 2: Develop a district- and/or school-level leadership team to guide implementation. A district leadership team should be formed to assess needs and develop a long-range plan (Horner & Sugai, 2000).

Membership should include representatives from each group of stakeholders, including district and building leadership, school psychologists and behavior specialists, school counselors, teachers, community leaders, and parents. A similar process should be followed at the school level. Each team will be responsible for decision making and implementation as appropriate.

Step 3: Assess and foster readiness for change. The leadership team should analyze district and/or school data related to student behavior. Teams should evaluate data such as the number of office discipline referrals and determine how behavioral problems are impacting their school.

Step 4: Develop a vision and promote teacher buy-in. Building principals and leadership teams should develop a vision for RTI at their school that promotes success for *all* students. Teachers should be given opportunities to voice and work through their concerns. The team should work toward a strong commitment from the faculty for full process implementation.

Step 5: Use data to make informed instructional decisions for all students. Teams will need to provide access to data through available technology. Both outcome and process data should drive the decision-making process.

Step 6: Provide strong staff development. Teachers and administrators will need ongoing training in a variety of areas. Some will need more extensive training for working with students with more severe behavioral problems.

Step 7: Engage in ongoing process evaluation. Leadership teams should continually assess program effectiveness and build capacity for stronger implementation. Yearly action plans should be developed and implemented.

Building a Strong Foundation Through Tier 1 Universal Supports

In the previous two chapters, discussion focused on process development for a comprehensive RTI model with specific emphasis on behavioral components. It is critical to take time to lay the groundwork for implementation. Once that is accomplished, leadership teams may begin developing each tier in order to provide appropriate instruction and support for all students. This also requires teams to lay a strong foundation by examining and strengthening the quality of Tier 1 instruction and behavior management. The effectiveness of subsequent tiers will rely heavily on the quality of Tier 1.

This chapter will focus on the quality of Tier 1 instruction and supports. It will include an overview of both academic and behavioral elements identified as best practices essential for quality instruction. Because academics and behavior are so closely connected, it is impossible to separate the two and still have effective instruction.

ESSENTIAL ELEMENTS OF TIER 1

As discussed in Chapter 1, Primary or Tier 1 supports provide effective instruction and behavior management that are available to all students within the school. Ultimately, Tier 1 support should be effective and sufficient for at least 80 percent of the student body (National Technical Assistance Center on Positive Behavioral Interventions and Supports, 2007; Vaughn & Roberts, 2007). In order to achieve this, it should include the components outlined in this section implemented with fidelity and consistency.

Quality Curriculum

In Tier 1 all students should have access to a quality curriculum. State standards should be taught with fidelity through the use of research-based curriculum materials and strategies. Instruction should be purposeful and well planned. In the elementary grades, reading instruction should be explicit and focus on phonemic awareness, phonics, fluency, vocabulary, and text comprehension (National Reading Panel [NRP], 2007). In the middle and high school grades, students must be able to comprehend written material in grade-level texts. They must have continued growth in the acquisition of complex written vocabulary, strategies for processing different kinds of text, conceptual and background knowledge, and reasoning and inferential skills (Greenwood, Kamps, Terry, & Linebarger, 2007). Math instruction in the elementary grades should focus on the critical foundations for algebra, namely proficiency with whole numbers, fractions, geometry, and measurement. As students enter middle and high school, they should master math skills in symbols and expressions, linear equations, quadratic equations, functions, algebra of polynomials, and finite probability (National Mathematics Advisory Panel [NMAP], 2008).

Aside from the academic curriculum, students must also be taught appropriate social skills and expectations for school behavior. A quality social skills curriculum should be taught with fidelity at all grade levels. Schools may use purchased materials and/or those developed by the state or district. The complexity of the curriculum will vary based on the needs of the school. Teams serving in schools with significant numbers of behavioral problems should choose a program that will offer explicit instruction and whose skills can be embedded in the general classroom instruction. The curriculum may focus on character education, violence and bullying prevention, drug abuse prevention, conflict resolution, and/or specific social skills instruction. It should be culturally responsive, taking into account the varied backgrounds of the students within the school. Again, the specific components of the chosen program should be based on the needs of the students.

The Collaborative for Academic, Social, and Emotional Learning (CASEL) is an excellent resource for guidance in choosing social skills curricula. CASEL provides guidelines, tools, and informational resources regarding evidence-based practices and programs for social and emotional learning. From CASEL's Web site, educators can access a document titled *Safe and Sound: An Educational Leader's Guide to Social and Emotional Learning Programs*. This guide presents evaluation results of more than eighty programs, including twenty that were designated as "CASEL Select" based on outstanding coverage in skill areas and quality of research (Collaborative for Academic, Social, and Emotional Learning [CASEL], 2007).

Table 3.1   Resources for Social Skills Curricula

Resource	Location
Collaborative for Academic, Social, and Emotional Learning (CASEL)	www.casel.org/programs/selecting.php
Boys Town Press	www.boystownpress.org
Academic and Social-Emotional Learning	www.ibe.unesco.org/publications/ EducationalPracticesSeriespdf/prac11e.pdf
Selecting Research-Based Prevention Programs for Your School	www.ed.gov/admins/lead/safety/training/selecting/ prevention_pg6.html
Social and Emotional Learning School Self-Assessment Guide	www.casel.org
Center for the Study and Prevention of Violence	www.colorado.edu/cspv
Character Education . . . Our Shared Responsibility	www.ed.gov/admins/lead/character/brochure.html
Safe, Disciplined, and Drug-Free Expert Panel Exemplary Programs 2001	www.ed.gov/admins/lead/safety/exemplary01/ exemplary01.pdf
Child Development Project	www.devstu.org/cdp/
Second Step Violence Prevention Project	www.cfchildren.org/programs/ssp/overview

Information about CASEL and other resources for choosing and evaluating social skills curricula is presented in Table 3.1.

Differentiated Instruction

After establishing a quality academic and social skills curriculum, instruction should be made appropriate for each student through effective use of differentiated instruction. This involves adjustments to content, process, and product according to the students' interests, abilities, and learning profiles. Students should be instructed at a level slightly above their instructional level. In this way, students are challenged but not overwhelmed by their assignments (Tomlinson, 1999).

Teachers often say they understand how to differentiate instruction, but find it difficult to actually carry it out in the classroom. They may even place students in various instructional groups, but all too often, all students are completing the same task in the same way. One of the most common methods for differentiating instruction involves varying assignments based on students' individual learning styles. For example, a teacher may allow a student to complete a book report by producing a written report, oral report, or writing and performing a song or skit. This style of differentiation is often easiest for teachers to incorporate into existing lesson plans.

However, differentiated instruction goes much deeper than adjusting for learning styles. It involves understanding students in a variety of ways and providing instruction that is explicitly designed to address their unique learning needs. In my experience training teachers in differentiated instructional practices, I find that a good place to begin adjusting instruction is by teaching to varied levels of complexity based on Bloom's Taxonomy (Bloom, 1984; Heacox, 2002). Through the use of informal and formal assessments, teachers should be able to identify students' functioning levels in the taxonomy: knowledge, comprehension, application, analysis, evaluation, and synthesis (see Figure 3.1). They may then adjust the content, process, and product based on these levels. In doing so, all students are given the amount of support they need while being challenged to higher levels.

Figure 3.1 Bloom's Taxonomy

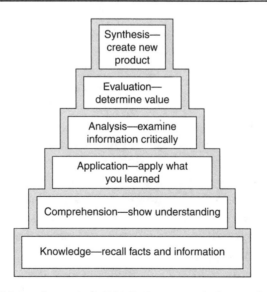

SOURCE: Adapted from Bloom, B. S. (1984). *Taxonomy of educational objectives: Book 1 cognitive domain*. Reading, MA: Addison-Wesley.

For example, Ms. Jackson teaches U.S. history. She is currently teaching the following standard: Students will identify key issues, events, and individuals relating to the causes, course, and consequences of the Civil War (Georgia Department of Education [GA DOE], 2008). Ms. Jackson administered a short preassessment to evaluate students' basic knowledge about the subject. She used the results to divide her class into three distinct groups. Group A scored 0–50 percent correct on the assessment. The members of this group displayed little or no knowledge about issues related to the Civil War. Group B scored 51–75 percent on the assessment, showing some basic understanding of the topic. Group C scored 76–90 percent on the assessment. These students showed a strong understanding of factual knowledge. Ms. Jackson used this information to develop several activities in her unit lesson plan (see Table 3.2).

In those activities, Groups A and B will receive direct instruction through lecture, videos, discussion, and computer software on the factual knowledge and application of the causes and consequences of the Civil War. Group A will complete graphic organizers in pairs to support their learning of the basic concepts. They will complete a matching and short answer test individually and develop a report in pairs using photos, written text, and presentation to the class. They may use a variety of resources to complete their work.

Group B will complete different graphic organizers that promote application and analysis of the causes and consequences of the Civil War. They will individually complete a multiformat test that includes short answer, essay questions, and vocabulary matching. They will develop a class presentation demonstrating application and analysis of the information. The presentation will be completed in pairs or alone (student's choice) and must include visuals, written text, and music or drama.

Group C will complete a Web-quest showing the long-term impact of the Civil War. They will write an essay or develop a PowerPoint presentation (student's choice) individually comparing the Civil War with the American Revolution.

Through these varied activities, each student will be challenged to high levels of thought and understanding. However, every student will meet the standard by demonstrating knowledge of causes and consequences of the Civil War. Ms. Jackson developed rubrics for each assignment that specified the content and format that was required. Students were graded based on their completion of the assignment and meeting the rubric requirements.

While it is true that units such as this one may require more preparation time than one prepared for the entire class, the benefit to the students is worthwhile and can be seen in both academic and behavioral

Table 3.2   Differentiated Lesson Plan

Assessment results and differentiated assignments

Group A—0–50% correct—little or no knowledge about causes and consequences of the Civil War

- Direct instruction through lecture, videos, and computer software
- Complete graphic organizers in pairs to support learning of basic concepts
- Complete matching and short answer test individually
- Develop report in pairs

Group B—51–75% correct—some basic understanding of the topic

- Direct instruction through lecture, videos, and computer software
- Complete graphic organizers to support application and analysis of causes and consequences of the Civil War
- Complete multi-format test individually
- Develop class presentation in pairs or alone (student's choice) demonstrating application and analysis of the information

Group C—76–90% correct—strong understanding of factual knowledge

- Complete a Web-quest showing long-term impact of Civil War
- Write essay or develop PowerPoint individually

---

performance. Children who exhibit problem behaviors are often trying to avoid some task that they consider unpleasant (Horner & Sugai, 2007a). We typically associate task avoidance with children who are unable to complete the assigned task due to lack of skills. However, this is not always the case. Avoidance behaviors can also occur when children are bored, disengaged, or receiving more reinforcement from an alternative task than from the assigned task (Sprick et al., 1998). Both of these issues are addressed when instruction is designed for and appropriate to meet individual student needs.

There are a multitude of excellent resources available on differentiating instruction. Teachers should receive ongoing training in concepts and strategies as well as technical assistance and classroom guidance in actual implementation. They should begin slowly by developing one unit or even one lesson that is differentiated in this way. After learning how to best organize and monitor instruction, they should feel more comfortable with the process and be able to plan in this way more often.

Administrators should monitor differentiated practices during classroom observations, lesson plan checks, and classroom walk-throughs. They may not see differentiated lessons daily, but should look for evidence on a weekly basis. Resource B contains an observation checklist and a

Table 3.3   Resources for Differentiated Instruction

Benjamin, A. (2002). *Differentiated instruction: A guide for middle and high school teachers.* Larchmont, NY: Eye on Education.

Chapman, C., & King, R. S. (2007). *Differentiated instructional management: Work smarter, not harder.* Thousand Oaks, CA: Corwin.

Gregory, G. H., & Chapman, C. (2006). *Differentiated instructional strategies: One size doesn't fit all.* Thousand Oaks, CA: Corwin.

Gregory, G. H., & Kuzmich, L. (2004). *Data driven differentiation in the standards-based classroom.* Thousand Oaks, CA: Corwin.

Heacox, D. (2002). *Differentiating instruction in the regular classroom: How to reach and teach all learners, grades 3–12.* Minneapolis, MN: Free Spirit Publishing.

Northey, S. (2005). *Handbook on differentiated instruction for middle and high schools.* Larchmont, NY: Eye on Education.

Thousand, J. S., Villa, R. A., & Nevin, A. I. (2007). *Differentiating instruction: collaborative planning and teaching for universally designed learning.* Thousand Oaks, CA: Corwin.

Tomlinson, C. A. (1999). *The differentiated classroom: Responding to the needs of all learners.* Alexandria, VA: Association for Supervision and Curriculum Development.

Tomlinson, C. A. (2003). *Fulfilling the promise of the differentiated classroom: Strategies and tools for responsive teaching.* Alexandria, VA: Association for Supervision and Curriculum Development.

Tomlinson, C. A. & Eidson, C. C. (2003). *Differentiation in practice: A resource guide for differentiating curriculum grades 5–9.* Alexandria, VA: Association for Supervision and Curriculum Development.

Tomlinson, C. A., & McTighe, J. (2006). *Integrating differentiated instruction and understanding by design.* Alexandria, VA: Association for Supervision and Curriculum Development.

Wiggins, G., & McTighe, J. (2005). *Understanding by design* (2nd ed.). Alexandria, VA: Association for Supervision and Curriculum Development.

---

lesson plan rubric for assessing implementation of differentiated instruction. In addition, Table 3.3 provides several resources on differentiated instruction to assist teachers in the process.

Formative and Summative Assessment

All quality instruction should be guided by student data. Chapter 2 contained a lengthy discussion about data in RTI process development. All subsequent chapters will discuss how outcome data are to be used to make instructional decisions as students proceed through the continuum of supports in Tiers 1, 2, and 3. However, it is equally important for teachers to use data to drive instruction for all students on a daily basis.

Formative assessment, both formal and informal, is used as an ongoing check of understanding for each student. It gives teachers immediate feedback on student understanding and mastery of information. Formative assessment can be easily accomplished through the use of simple tools such as informal questioning and response, brief quizzes, homework review, and exit cards (also called tickets out the door) for both individuals and groups. Formative tools should be administered as often as weekly or daily to keep the teacher informed of every child's progress. Teachers should systematically assess individual student strengths and weaknesses and use that information to adjust instruction. As weakness areas are identified, teachers should adjust and differentiate instruction further, providing additional supports and remediation as needed. Assessment results should also be used to place students into flexible groups according to their ability, interests, learning style, or other appropriate identifiers.

Summative assessment also plays an important role in raising student achievement. It can have the greatest impact when test data is analyzed to identify and correct weaknesses in curriculum, instruction, and supports. Assessment tools such as chapter tests, end-of-course tests, and criterion or norm-referenced tests yield a wealth of information that is most effectively used in long-range planning. It complements, but cannot take the place of, formative assessment. For example, teachers should never be surprised by their students' performance on unit tests. If they have used formative assessment throughout the teaching of the unit, they should be able to accurately predict most students' final scores. Without formative assessment teachers may be very surprised by students' outcomes and become frustrated over their inability to go back and teach missed information. Balancing formative and summative assessment allows teachers to adjust instruction as necessary to maximize student learning.

Formative assessment for measuring behavior also involves ongoing assessment and adjustment of instruction. In Tier 1 administrators or data teams should carefully monitor student behavior. This may be accomplished by frequently observing students in the common areas of the school and may involve the use of a rubric to document compliance with expectations. It may also involve frequent review of office discipline referrals. Teams should analyze the data to determine which expectations need to be reviewed or retaught. Teachers may then embed the review and reteaching in their daily instruction and/or teach explicit lessons on the deficit skills. The same process applies to individual classrooms in which teachers keep track of all student behaviors and review and reteach expectations as needed. Teachers should develop a simple data management system, perhaps at least partially completed by the students. This may be modeled after the previously mentioned form in Resource B.

Summative assessment for behavior may involve a review every grading period, semester, or school year. It most often involves a summative review of office discipline referrals, as outlined in the previous chapter. Teams should consider not only the number of referrals, but also specifics such as locations, times of day that misbehavior most frequently occurs, and categories of behavior incidences. This will help the leadership team make adjustments to various parts of the school-wide management plan, such as developing more manageable traffic patterns or determining the need for additional supervision at various times or in different locations. At the classroom level, teachers can easily see which components of their classroom management plan are most effective and which ones need to be changed. They may identify transition periods that need more structure, locations in the room that need to be more visible, or students who need to be separated.

When leadership teams and teachers use formative and summative assessment to guide academic and behavioral instruction, they can make appropriate changes before problems become unmanageable. In reading, formative assessment allows teachers to provide additional or different instruction at the earliest signs of deficit. It accomplishes the same task when used with behavior management. Summative assessment is most helpful in long-range planning and works to strengthen instruction and management for both academics and behavior. Schools should strive for a balance of the two in order to make the most efficient and effective instruction available to students.

Backward Design

As teachers become more skilled at using data to adjust instruction, they may begin to use their focus on assessment as the core of planning and instruction. This is the premise behind a planning process known as Backward Design (Wiggins & McTighe, 2005). This process begins lesson planning with the end result clearly defined. Teachers determine what they want their students to *know*, *do*, and *understand* at the end of an instructional unit and the types of evidence (assignments or tasks) that will demonstrate their learning. For example, a teacher may plan for his students to silently read a prose passage. He may determine that students will *know* the main idea, supporting facts, and the resolution or outcome. The students will answer comprehension questions at the end of the story (*do*). Finally, the students will discuss the theme of the story and apply it to a new situation by writing their own stories with similar themes (*understand*).

Once the teacher has identified each of these components, he pre-assesses his students to determine their present level of knowledge and then develops lessons and activities that will lead students to the desired level of knowledge and understanding. By beginning with the outcome in mind, teachers can be sure that they teach everything the student needs to know in order to arrive at the desired goal. They can effectively pace their instruction and spend more time and resources on the most important concepts.

Backward Design can be applied to behavioral instruction as well. Teachers should begin by identifying behavioral goals they want their students to meet by the end of the instructional period—the grading period, semester, or school year. These goals should clearly articulate what students should know, do, and understand (Sprick et al., 1998). For example, a teacher may determine that she wants her students to be able to work cooperatively in groups. Preassessment may involve a ten-minute cooperative learning activity assessed through a rubric for working together. She will then analyze the results to determine what students need to know, do, and understand differently in order for them to be successful with group work. Table 3.4 outlines the teacher's specific expectations for accomplishing this goal. Once these expectations are clarified, the teacher designs brief social skills lessons to teach them to her students. These lessons are incorporated into her directions for beginning assignments. She may also develop assessments such as peer rating tools and/or self-checks to monitor progress toward these goals (see Tables 3.5 and 3.6).

By having a clear picture of desired behavioral results, teachers can plan systematic, explicit instruction that focuses on those results. Students receive behavior instruction instead of behavior management alone. This greatly increases the likelihood that students will meet expectations. As a result, behavior management is less complex and requires less of the teacher's attention and time.

Table 3.4   Expectations for Cooperative Group Work

- Work as a team.
  - Each person should contribute ideas.
  - Each person should value the contributions of others.
- Listen while others are talking.
- Assign tasks to each group member.
- Stay on task. Conversation should be limited to the project.
- Complete assignments on time.
- Keep noise levels low so that only your group members can hear.
- Complete self-assessment and peer-assessment after project is completed.

Table 3.5   Peer Evaluation Tool for Cooperative Groups

Task	Always	Most of the Time	Some of the Time	Never
Every person in the group performed a job				
Every person in the group contributed ideas				
Every person in the group helped to keep the assignment on task				
Every person in the group controlled their behavior				

If you answered "some of the time" or "never" to any of these items, please explain.

_____

_____

_____

_____

_____

_____

_____

_____

_____

_____

_____

_____

_____

_____

_____

_____

Table 3.6   Self-Check Tool for Cooperative Groups

Task	Always	Most of the Time	Some of the Time	Never
I did my best on this task				
I contributed ideas to the group				
I understood the requirements of the task				
I learned the information that was presented				
I thought this activity was worthwhile				

If you answered "some of the time" or "never" to any of the items, please explain.

_____

_____

_____

_____

_____

_____

_____

_____

_____

_____

_____

_____

_____

_____

_____

Behavioral Plans

A key component of quality Tier 1 instruction is effective school-wide and classroom management. This is true even in RTI models that only provide academic supports. However, in a comprehensive RTI model, it provides the foundation for all other supports and must be accessible for all students. Tier 1 supports are built on the idea that schools should not ignore students who are currently not engaging in problem behaviors. These supports provide systematic methods for training, monitoring, and reinforcing students in universal expectations and behaviors (Sugai, Sprague et al., 2000). Therefore, a great deal of time and effort should be devoted to data analysis and plan development. The end result should be an objective and proactive plan that will enable approximately 80 percent of students to be successful. Schools that have more than 2.5 office discipline referrals (ODRs) per student, more than 8 ODRs per day, or that have more than 45 percent of their students receive one or more ODRs in a school year need to focus on strengthening Tier 1 universal supports (McIntosh et al., 2006; Sugai, Sprague, et al., 2000).

Effective school-wide behavioral plans should prevent problem behaviors by focusing on all students across all settings (OSEP Center on Positive Behavioral Interventions and Supports, 2004). They should pay close attention to antecedent factors, defined as events that prompt or trigger both appropriate and inappropriate behaviors. As leadership teams begin to develop a school-wide behavioral plan, they should follow a sequential process for clearly establishing all relevant factors.

Initially, teams should reexamine behavioral data used in process development to identify and prioritize the specific behavioral issues to be addressed by the plan. Formative and summative assessment data, as discussed previously, will reveal the most common and most critical areas in need of intervention. The social skills curriculum should reflect these areas.

Establishing School-Wide Guidelines

Next, the team should use this information to identify behavioral expectations across settings and for a variety of activities, including transitions. They should lead the faculty in developing a set of four or five guidelines that will be expected in all areas of the school. It is important for students to understand that (1) the same behaviors are expected in all areas of the school and (2) all staff members expect and will reinforce the guidelines. Some schools work the guidelines into an acronym or slogan to assist students in remembering them. The expectations should be posted throughout the school, in classrooms, and in student handbooks or agendas. They should be broad enough to cover a variety of settings and

Table 3.7 Expectations for Middle School

	Cooperate	Act With Appropriate Attitude	Take Responsibility	Show Respect
Classroom	• Follow directions the first time • Stay on task • Speak appropriately • Follow rules • Stay in assigned area	• Show eagerness to learn • Speak positively toward both teachers and students	• Bring all needed materials • Be prepared • Complete all assignments on time • Keep classroom area clean	• Leave property of others alone • Respect personal space
Hallway	• Keep hands, feet, and objects to yourself • Leave room for others to pass	• Keep hallway clean • Keep lockers and walls clean	• Have a signed agenda/pass during class time • Stay in designated area	• Keep hands, feet, and objects away from others, walls, and displays • Use quiet voices • Walk on right side of hallway

situations. All staff members should reinforce the guidelines in their classrooms and in all activities (OSEP Center on Positive Behavioral Interventions and Supports, 2004; Sprick et al., 1998). Table 3.7 gives an example of school expectations or guidelines for classrooms and hallways in a middle school. Resource B contains the full matrix of school-wide guidelines specified for each area of the school.

Setting Rules

In addition to the broad school-wide guidelines, teachers should establish classroom rules that are more specific and give additional guidance to students regarding behavioral expectations. In general, the most effective sets of rules consist of four or five positively worded statements. The required behaviors should be objective and observable. Be polite is a broad guideline. Listen while others are speaking is a more specific rule (Janney & Snell, 2008; Marzano, Marzano, & Pickering, 2003; Sprick et al., 1998). Table 3.8 provides an example of rules that might be appropriate in an elementary setting.

These rules are designed to create a positive learning environment within the general education classroom. Research shows that effective teachers establish rules and expectations at the beginning of the school

Table 3.8   Rules for Elementary School

- Be respectful of others.
- Be respectful of our time.
- Be respectful of our space.
- Be respectful of our materials.

year and consistently apply them throughout the year (Conroy, Sutherland, Snyder, & Marsh, 2008). In the absence of rules, students are more likely to display aggressive and disruptive behaviors (H. Walker, Colvin, & Ramsey, 1995).

Clarifying and Teaching Expectations

Once school expectations and classroom rules have been established, they should be overtly taught to students in all grade levels (Conroy et al., 2008; Fairbanks, Sugai, Guardino, & Lathrop, 2007). Students must understand what each expectation and rule looks like and sounds like in the classroom, in common areas in the school (cafeteria, hallways, media center, playground) and for all major transitions (class change, locker break, restroom breaks). The instruction should consist of discussion of the expectations, modeling, and practice. These expectations should be integrated into the social skills curriculum and taught at the beginning of the school year, after each major holiday, and as students have difficulty following them (Lohrmann-O'Rourke et al., 2000; Sprick et al., 1998).

This same process should be applied in each classroom (Fairbanks et al., 2007). It is important to remember that every teacher has different expectations for issues, such as how students should request help and when it is okay to talk with another student. Each teacher should spend time thinking about and clarifying for himself his own expectations for the variety of activities within the day, such as small group work, whole group instruction, independent work, etc. Once he has clarified expectations in his own mind, he can be much more consistent when managing student behavior. If expectations are directly taught for each class activity and for transition times, students should have no question about what is acceptable (Janney & Snell, 2008; Sprick et al., 1998).

After establishing the expectations, teachers should continue to review or reteach them until students consistently follow them for each activity. If the explicit teaching is diminished before achieving compliance on a regular basis, students will assume they have met the expectations. They should be reviewed after extended vacation periods and when students slip in their compliance. The expectations may be displayed in the room to make quick reviews easier (Sprick et al., 1998).

CHAMPs: A Proactive and Positive Approach to Classroom Management (Sprick et al., 1998) is an excellent resource for school teams and individual teachers to use for this process. This book provides assistance to teachers as they establish clear expectations for both classroom and transition activities and then teach the expectations to their students. It is organized into modules that walk teachers through the steps of clarifying and teaching expectations. Numerous worksheets and planning forms offer guiding questions that lead teachers through the development of a classroom management plan. It also contains multiple tools for monitoring and revising classroom plans based on student data. A follow-up book titled *Discipline in the Secondary Classroom* (Sprick, 2006) provides similar assistance to schools and teachers in Grades 9–12.

Many schools have developed school-wide guidelines, and most teachers have clearly stated rules in their classrooms. However, the effect of each is often diminished because the next step of directly teaching expectations is left out. The tendency for many teachers is to say they do not have time to overtly teach behavioral expectations and assess compliance. This explicit instruction may seem to take more time from academics than the teacher feels she can give. However, this argument negates the strong link between academics and behavior that has been previously established. Implementing proactive behavioral instruction increases time on task and reduces disciplinary referrals. In the long run, time invested in explicit behavioral instruction will pay off in more time devoted to academic instruction.

Establishing Routines

After expectations have been taught, teachers should establish consistent routines that are easily applied to multiple events and settings (Marzano et al., 2003; Sprick et al., 1998). For example, a specific routine should be developed for turning in homework. With this routine students should know exactly where and when to turn in their work. Consistency will help all students, especially those who have poor organizational skills. Routines are also helpful for beginning and ending class, gathering materials for class, and recording assignments. Once routines are established, it is very important to consistently follow them. Inconsistency is often more detrimental to behavioral plans than never having established the routines at all.

Routines are also important in the school-wide plan. The leadership team should examine the daily schedule and recurring activities and develop routine procedures for each one. For example, most schools have a time for school-wide announcements, the Pledge of Allegiance, or a moment of silence. This activity happens at the same time every day. Students know that the expected behavior for the routine is to be quiet for announcements and stand for the Pledge. This same consistency should be applied to other activities such as arrival and departure time, visiting the school store, and going to the restroom during class. However, the routines are only effective if followed by every student and enforced by every staff member. If one teacher allows students to go to the restroom without a hall pass, the routine and expectations are no longer effective.

Rewards and Incentives

A concept central to positive behavioral plans and RTI is the need for a system of rewards and incentives for students (Janney & Snell, 2008). When discussing this topic with educators, I am occasionally told that students should not be rewarded for doing the right thing or that rewards are nothing more than bribes.

I strongly disagree. Members of the adult workforce rely heavily on a rewards system. Incentives include vacation time, bonuses, insurance, and, of course, salary. There are few teachers and administrators who would come to work each day if they knew there would be no paycheck at the end of the month. School climate always improves when teachers are shown sincere appreciation for the jobs they do, even if that appreciation is only a verbal "thank you." Why, then, should we expect students to be completely self-motivated and not need the same types of rewards?

In reality very few students are self-motivated. The reasons for this are varied. Some begin school with an internal drive to learn and succeed, but experience failure early on. Basically, these children find that the amount of effort they put into a task has little to do with the outcome. They may work their hardest and fail miserably. After a while they decide that they are no longer willing to put forth effort for negative results (Lavoie, 2007).

Other students may receive more reinforcement for noncompliance than for compliance. For example, students who are seeking attention from peers or adults often don't care whether the attention they receive is positive or negative. They just need attention and therefore do whatever it takes to gain it. In other instances a student may prefer to sleep rather than do his work. He gets more reinforcement from the sleep than from the work. In fact, there may be no reward for completing the work, and therefore it is an easy choice.

The list could go on and on. In later sections we will discuss the purpose or function of behavior and the importance of determining that purpose. However, for our current discussion it is important for the reader to understand that intrinsic motivation is insufficient as an incentive or reward for most students. Therefore, it is imperative that schools develop a reward system and consistently apply it.

There are a variety of ways to provide a reward system. Most schools involved in School-Wide Positive Behavior Interventions and Supports programs use a form of token economy in which students earn tokens or tickets that may be traded for a variety of tangible and intangible rewards. Tickets are given for various reasons, including compliance with school-wide guidelines and classroom rules, demonstrating appropriate behavior, or showing improvement in academics or behavior.

These rewards do not have to involve large amounts of funding. Schools seem to find very inventive ways to motivate their students. For example, a middle school scheduled a school-wide pep rally to celebrate their reduction in office discipline referrals. As part of the pep rally, several teachers and administrators volunteered to allow students to throw whipped cream pies at them. Students were allowed to place tickets in a basket with each volunteer's name. During the pep rally, several students' tickets were drawn from each basket. These students won the opportunity to throw a pie.

If there is a budget for rewards or if the school can get sponsorships or donations from local businesses, students may earn prizes such as bicycles, radios, skateboards, or other items of interest. Rather than giving to the student with the most tickets, many schools hold silent auctions in which students place bids for particular items using their tickets. Tickets are then drawn for the winner. In this way even students with few tickets have an opportunity to win the auction. However, the more tickets in the box, the greater the chance of winning.

There are several important factors to keep in mind when establishing incentive programs. First and foremost, the incentives must be of interest to the students. Leadership teams may choose to give incentive surveys or interest inventories as part of their data collection to assist in choosing appropriate reward systems. Secondly, the criteria for earning rewards must be attainable for the majority of students. Rewards should be available for meeting short-term and long-term goals. Many students are motivated by the promise of a field trip at the end of a six-week period. However, for some students that time span is overwhelming and seems completely unattainable. For them, other incentives must be available. Table 3.9 contains examples of rewards and incentives that are appropriate for students at various grade levels. Resource B contains a Rewards Menu developed for use at the middle school level. These should be considered a starting point as teams work to develop incentives based on their students' preferences and interests.

Table 3.9   Reward Menu Appropriate for Various Grade Levels (Cats Cash)

Patio Pass—15 Cats Cash (CC) per student

Used only on a day when it is not raining or wet outside. This day will be designated each month and will be announced. Student must give Cats Cash to teacher he or she has for lunch prior to going to the patio to eat. A staff member would need to be outside to supervise. Students are to remain seated at the tables while outside. All trash must be collected and disposed of when coming inside.

Eat Lunch With a Friend in Lunchroom—10 CC

Student must give Cats Cash to teacher and get teacher's approval before sitting with a friend at a table other than the one assigned. Students must follow all lunchroom expectations while at the friend's table. Student must leave with his/her regular class.

Teacher's Aide—15 CC

This must be arranged at least a day before it is to occur. The teacher of the class the student is missing and the teacher who the student wants to aid must approve beforehand in writing. Student must give Cats Cash to teacher of the class he or she is missing. Student is required to make up any missed work from the class.

Hat Day Pass—10 CC

This item is only available on designated hat days, not every school day. Student must give Cats Cash to the teacher who is collecting money for the hat day sticker.

Athletic Event Pass—15 CC

This item is only available at home events. Student must give Cats Cash to the teacher who is collecting money at the gate of the event.

Activity in Gym During Homeroom—10 CC

This will occur on a designated day each month and will be announced letting everyone know when it will occur. Student must give Cats Cash to homeroom teacher and get teacher's approval and pass before going to the gym. The pass must be presented when entering the back door of the gym.

Demerit Pass—20 CC

Students may eliminate a demerit by giving the Cats Cash to the teacher when the demerit is being issued. The demerit form will still be completed by the teacher noting the behavior infraction and will be filed with the redeemed Cats Cash attached by the student's team leader for data purposes.

Outside Reward Time—15 CC

This will occur on a designated day each month and will be announced letting everyone know when it will occur. This will occur during team time and each team will determine when they will go outside. Student must give Cats Cash to homeroom teacher to participate.

Dance Pass—15 CC

This item may be used to gain admittance into any of the scheduled school-wide dances. Student should give the Cats Cash to the person collecting the money at the entrance to the auxiliary gym.

Late Homework Pass—5 CC

This item can be redeemed on a day that a homework assignment is due. The student must complete a Late Homework Pass form, staple the Cats Cash to the form, and turn the form into the teacher that day in class. The student then has three school days to turn in the completed homework assignment with no late points being deducted.

Pay Media Center Fine—1 CC

A student may redeem Cats Cash to pay a media center fine. For this reward 1 Cats Cash is equivalent to $.25 worth of library fines. Student must present the Cats Cash to the media center staff.

Pencil Purchase—2 CC

Some teachers may allow a student to redeem Cats Cash for a pencil if they are unprepared. The student can present the Cats Cash to the teacher for a pencil. If the student does not have Cats Cash, the teacher may loan them a pencil but will make a checkmark in their records. If a student receives three checkmarks from the teacher in a nine-week grading period, the student will receive a demerit for being unprepared. The student will also receive a demerit for each additional checkmark until the end of that grading period.

Locker Pass—2 CC

Some teachers may allow a student to redeem Cats Cash in order to go to their locker to get school-related items that they need for class purposes. Student must ask the teacher if they can go back to their locker to get said item(s) and must then pay the Cats Cash to the teacher.

School Store Items—Varying CC

Students may purchase school store items when the store is open. The amount of Cats Cash needed to purchase will vary depending on the item. Student should give the Cats Cash to the staff member running the store.

Gift Card Drawing—1 CC

Instead of redeeming Cats Cash for the above reward items, students may have their Cats Cash entered into a weekly drawing for a $25 gift card of their choice. This drawing will occur every Friday during morning announcements. Students can enter as many Cats Cash as they wish thus increasing their odds of winning. During the last week of each grading period there will be three $100 gift card winners drawn. In this drawing there will be one winner from each grade level.

ALL ITEMS ARE SUBJECT TO TEACHER DISCRETION

Several years ago I worked with a school that was reporting little success with their support program. When I asked about their rewards, they explained that students who received no demerits for the entire week were given free popcorn on Friday during lunch. This scenario presents several factors that are contrary to positive behavioral plans. First, the management system was based on giving negative consequences (demerits) rather than providing positive incentives. Secondly, their time frame was too long. There were no incremental goals or rewards for students and no ways to earn back the privilege. If a student received a demerit on Monday, he had to wait an entire week for another opportunity for a reward. Therefore, his behavior for the remainder of the week often continued to worsen. Finally, the reward of free popcorn was inadequate compensation for the stringent requirements. The school had failed to consider the interests of the students, and therefore had chosen an ineffective motivator. My advice to the faculty was to reevaluate their practices and develop a system based on positive reinforcers and student interests.

Developing Consequences

The final component of a successful behavioral plan, at both the school and classroom levels, is the development of consequences for noncompliance with rules and expectations (Janney & Snell, 2008). When paired with appropriate rewards for positive behavior, appropriate consequences can significantly increase most students' compliance with rules and expectations.

Teams should consider appropriate consequences for a student's failure to follow the school-wide expectations. Consequences should be as mild as possible and still produce the desired effect. Two or three additional consequences should follow a continuum, becoming increasingly more restrictive with each step. One mistake that educators often make is starting with consequences that are too severe or moving from very mild to very severe with nothing in between. This may cause the teacher to be inconsistent in applying the consequences (Sprick et al., 1998). Resource B contains an example of a school's plan for multi-leveled consequences based on the intensity of the behavior problem.

A successful behavioral plan for school-wide and classroom management can be developed by carefully considering and following each of the steps outlined above and summarized in Table 3.10. This plan should be designed so that behavior management is easy for all staff members to implement consistently. It forms the foundation of the Tier 1 structure and impacts the success of interventions in Tiers 2 and 3. It should be considered a fluid plan that grows and changes with the needs and interests of the students.

Table 3.10   Steps in Developing School-Wide and Classroom Management Plan

1. Establish school-wide guidelines.
2. Establish age appropriate rules.
3. Clarify and teach expectations.
4. Establish routines.
5. Establish rewards and incentives.
6. Develop consequences.

As noted throughout this section, Resource B contains examples of many of these elements designed for school-wide implementation. Examples include a Behavior Matrix, which establishes guidelines and expectations for all locations within the school; Rewards Menu; description of Behavior Levels based on intensity; and Discipline Referral Form.

Universal Screening and Data-Based Decision Making

Our next component of Tier 1 is that of universal screening for the identification of nonresponders. To assess academic functioning, this is most often in the form of benchmark testing which compares a student's performance with that of his peers or an established benchmark.

Academic universal screening tools may be norm-referenced or criterion-referenced. Norm-referenced tools compare an individual's performance with that of his peer group. For example, a student may be compared to all other students in his class or grade. The results usually place the student at a percentile rank. A student who scores at the 25th percentile has performed as well as or better than 25 percent of the compared group (Mellard & Johnson, 2008).

Criterion-referenced assessment tools compare an individual's performance with a standard or benchmark. For example, third-grade students may be expected to multiply multi-digit math problems with 75 percent accuracy. Students who are unable to meet this criterion are considered at risk and in need of intervention.

There are many examples of norm-referenced and criterion-referenced assessments used throughout the United States. Some of these are state mandated to meet assessment requirements for No Child Left Behind accountability. Schools sometimes use these tools as one universal measure for RTI. However, in order to continually assess students for ongoing intervention needs, additional measures that can be implemented several times during the year must be identified.

There are numerous such screening tools on the market for reading, and a smaller number for math. These tools assess basic skills such as reading fluency, reading comprehension, and math problem solving. They require minimal time from the teacher and students and can be given multiple times in one school year. Teams will find a comprehensive listing in a tools chart located at www.studentprogress.org. In addition, districts and schools may develop their own assessments based on state criteria or local benchmarks.

The purpose of these tools is to identify which students are not making adequate progress. A cut-point is the demarcation line in the universal screening tool that identifies if a student is at risk for failure, or in the case of behavior, in need of targeted interventions. In an academic model, the cut-point may be an established benchmark, such as an Oral Reading Fluency score of 120 words per minute, or a percentile, such as the lowest 20 percent of the class. Students falling below the cut-point are considered for Tier 2 interventions.

When assessing behavior, universal screening and the cut-points to identify at-risk students are not as clearly defined. As discussed previously, schools often look to the number of office discipline referrals (ODRs) as an indicator of at-risk students. One problem associated with using ODR for universal screening is the possible lack of consistency between staff members in using these referrals for similar situations. Some teachers have different expectations for student behavior or have a much higher tolerance for misbehavior. Some may refer students to the office for minor offenses while others only do so as a last resort. Sugai and colleagues (2000) defined an office discipline referral as an event in which

1. a student exhibited a behavior that violated a school rule or expectation;
2. the behavior was observed or identified by a staff member; and
3. the student was given a consequence by administrative staff that resulted in a written record of the event. (Sugai, Sprague, et al., 2000, p. 96)

Schools may further clarify appropriate referrals by listing certain events, such as aggression toward others, as being an appropriate prereferral event. Resource B contains an example of a Discipline Referral Form developed by a school staff based on their School-Wide Positive Behavior Supports process. It distinguishes between Level 2 and 3 behaviors, as outlined in the description of Behavior Levels. This helps to clarify for all staff members what is considered an appropriate referral. In addition, districts may increase the reliability of their data by conducting ongoing staff development to train teachers and administrators in criteria that constitutes an appropriate referral and in discriminating between behavior that does and does not warrant a referral (McIntosh et al., 2006).

When referrals are defined and used consistently, ODR data is considered to be a good indication of the overall effectiveness of a behavioral plan and of individual student compliance (Sugai, Sprague, et al., 2000). By sixth grade ODR is a reliable predictor of future chronic discipline problems, violent events in school, and tendency to drop out of school (Tobin & Sugai, 1999). In addition, ODR is highly correlated with social maladjustment and juvenile delinquency (Irvin, Tobin, Sprague, Sugai, & Vincent, 2004). This data is also a good indicator for children at risk of developing emotional and behavioral problems in the future (B. Walker et al., 2005). Therefore, it is the most commonly used universal screening tool for identifying students in need of Tier 2 interventions (Sugai, Sprague, et al., 2000).

When using office discipline referrals for this purpose, the typical cutpoint identifies a student with 0 to 1 ODR as one who is making adequate progress with Tier 1 practices. Students with 2 to 5 ODRs are considered to be in need of Tier 2 targeted interventions, and students with 6 or more are considered appropriate for Tier 3 (Walker, Cheney, Stage, & Blum, 2005).

However, ODR is only reliable as a predictor for externalizing behaviors such as noncompliance, aggression, and disruption. Students with internalizing behaviors such as withdrawal, depression, worry, fear, and anxiety are seldom identified if this is the only screening tool used. Other screening tools that have good reliability and validity can be used to more appropriately identify all students in need of targeted interventions. Some of these tools identify students who currently exhibit behavioral problems, while others identify students with risk factors that might indicate future behavior problems. Together these tools can reliably predict students in need of supports beyond Tier 1.

Walker and colleagues (B. Walker et al., 2005) used a school-wide screening tool called Systematic Screening for Behavior Disorders (SSBD; H. Walker & Severson, 1992) to supplement ODR data. This tool was found to be reliable and valid for identifying students with externalizing and internalizing behaviors. It involves three stages: Stage 1—teacher nomination, Stage 2—critical events inventory and behavior checklist, and Stage 3—observations. Students who are identified in Stage 2 are considered to be in need of Tier 2 interventions. The researchers found that this instrument coupled with ODR allowed schools to identify a broader population of at-risk students that included children with both externalizing and internalizing behaviors (Sprague et al., 2001).

Another universal screening tool is the Strengths and Difficulties Questionnaire (SDQ; Goodman, 1997, as cited in Lane, Parks, Kalberg, & Carter, 2007). It has been validated for use in Grades K–12 and is considered a valid and reliable tool for predicting risk for behavioral problems. However, the tool requires teachers to complete a twenty-five-item checklist for every student in the class, which can be quite time-consuming (Lane, Parks, et al., 2007).

An alternative tool that was shown to closely correlate with the SDQ is the Student Risk Screening Scale (SRSS; Drummond, 1994). This one-page, seven-item checklist completed by a student's teacher was found to be psychometrically sound for identifying students in Grades K–6 who are at risk for antisocial behavior. It was also found to correlate strongly with the Aggressive Behavior Subscale of the Child Behavior Checklist (CBCL; Achenbach, 1991), a more involved tool commonly used to identify students with emotional behavioral disorders. SRSS is considered to be more feasible for class-wide screening because of its brevity (fifteen minutes for assessing the entire class) and the ease with which it can be summarized and interpreted by behavioral teams (Lane, Parks, et al., 2007). It may be downloaded at no cost from www.sch-psych.net/archive/000808.php.

When choosing universal screening tools, schools should supplement ODR data with systematic universal screening such as the SSBD or SRSS, along with frequent monitoring of classrooms and student social functioning. This combination of tools and data can effectively identify students with internalizing and externalizing behaviors so that schools may provide early interventions and supports prior to the emergence of significant behavioral problems (B. Walker et al., 2005).

An important point to remember about universal screening tools is that they must be feasible for use with an entire school. A feasible screener is one that is inexpensive, quick, and requires limited personnel and resources to administer, score, and analyze (Lane, Parks, et al., 2007). Data teams should analyze individual student data from universal screening tools when determining who needs Tier 2 or 3 interventions. It is very helpful to look at students with multiple referrals to determine the existence of behavior patterns in terms of setting, time of day, peer group, frequency, and duration. This will be essential in developing individual intervention plans. Whenever teams are evaluating behavior patterns of individual students, it is important to ensure that the student has had access to Tier 1 practices that have proven effective for the majority of students. If this cannot be substantiated, teams should explore the quality of Tier 1 instruction before making individual intervention plans (Sandomierski et al., 2007).

As indicated earlier, it is very important for schools to have a system for managing and tracking student data. Software that disaggregates school discipline records allows teams to examine school-wide and individual data to determine the effectiveness of programs and to identify students in need of additional interventions. Many programs allow schools to designate their own cut-points and criteria for referral to Tier 2. Several of these programs were discussed in Chapter 2.

Fidelity of Implementation

As leadership teams develop their Tier 1 processes, they should determine the procedures that will be used to ensure fidelity of implementation. Even the best plans, if not implemented with consistency and integrity, will prove unsuccessful.

Monitoring fidelity of instruction and implementation can take several forms. Administrators may check teachers' lesson plans to verify the presence of differentiated instruction, core curricular concepts, backward design, and formative and summative assessment. A rubric that outlines essential components can make this process quick and efficient. One such rubric that can be used for lesson plans or direct observations can be found in Resource B.

In addition, administrators should frequently observe instruction in all classrooms. This may be done through both formal observations and short walk-throughs. Observers should ensure that both the academic and behavioral curricula are being taught correctly and consistently. They should also determine if behavioral expectations and procedures are being implemented appropriately. This may be documented through brief checklists. A digital tool called E-Walk is also available for this purpose. Developed by Media-x Systems, E-Walk allows observers to collect data across multiple observations for documentation of appropriate instruction. It is a Web-based system that uses templates designed to match the purpose of the observation. Information about E-Walk is available at www.media-x.com/products/ewalk/index.php.

Leadership teams must also spend time evaluating school-wide data. As plans are implemented, teams should analyze trends to determine the effectiveness of the overall plan. Careful examination of data from multiple years should reveal significant decreases in office discipline referrals and other problem-behavior indicators. This information should be used to revise the school-wide plan each year.

Finally, leadership teams should carefully monitor the appropriateness and contextual fit of the behavioral plan within the school. Data teams should carefully analyze process data to continually adjust and refine the RTI plan. The School-Wide Evaluation Tool and Benchmarks of Quality were discussed at length in Chapter 2. These tools will assist teams in determining how well the school-wide plan is being implemented and is working. As discussed in Chapter 2, this is the equivalent of progress monitoring for the school. It will reveal which areas are working well and which need modification.

EXAMPLE OF TIER 1 IN A COMPREHENSIVE RTI MODEL

Willow Oaks Middle School is located in a suburb of Atlanta, Georgia. The school has approximately 1,000 students in Grades 6–8. Dr. Davis has been principal at the school for six years.

At the beginning of the 2004–2005 school year, a leadership team was formed at Willow Oaks for the purpose of developing a comprehensive RTI model to address student achievement and behavioral deficits. After a year of planning and preparation, the model was implemented in the fall of 2005. Willow Oak's plan is a three-tiered system of interventions and supports for academics and behavior. The major components of its RTI model are outlined in Table 3.11.

In the 2007–2008 school year, 87 percent of students met standards in reading, 84 percent met standards in math, and 91 percent of students received 0 to 1 office discipline referrals. Willow Oaks has experienced consistent decreases in problem behaviors during each year of implementation. The leadership team regularly analyzes school-wide data as illustrated in Table 3.12 and Figure 3.2. Using the School-Wide Information System (SWIS), they are able to analyze referrals by staff member, problem behavior, location, time, and student. These data are used to develop new RTI implementation plans each school year. Table 3.12 illustrates how many referrals were made during each month for three school years. Teams may use this information to identify trends across the school year. In months that traditionally have higher numbers of referrals, they may choose to adjust or implement additional components of the behavioral plan.

Figure 3.2 was created by the leadership team to compare referrals during the 2008–2009 school year with those made in past years. As you can see, the school experienced a significant increase in August referrals (school began on August 7) when compared with previous years. This

Table 3.11   Components of Willow Oaks Middle School's RTI Plan

	Academic	Behavior
Quality Curriculum	• State performance standards taught to all students • Differentiated instruction used in all classrooms • Backward Design is used as a planning tool • Informal formative assessment tools are consistently used to drive instruction	• State character education curriculum taught to all students • Backward Design is used as a planning tool • School-wide expectations are outlined in student handbook, explicitly taught to students during weekly advisement period, and reinforced throughout the school year • Consistent set of classroom rules and routines are applied in all classrooms
Universal Screening	• State mandated test results from spring are used for fall assessment • Benchmark assessment tools based on state standards are administered in November and April	• Office discipline referrals • Student Risk Screening Scale (Drummond, 1994) completed for all students by homeroom teacher (downloaded from www.sch-psych.net/archive/000808.php)
Data-Based Decision Making	• Data is used to design staff development, identify curriculum gaps in instruction and/or materials, and identify teachers in need of support • Data is used to identify students who need additional supports	• Data is used to refine school-wide management plan, identify instructional gaps, identify teachers in need of support, and identify setting events which precipitate most behavioral problems. • Data is used to identify students who need additional supports.
Rewards and Incentives	• Student of Excellence program • Item from Reward Menu for students on A or A/B honor roll • Tickets to be used in "CATS" program for earning a grade of A or B on test or quiz • Reward Menu for cashing in tickets	• Student of the Month program • Item from Reward Menu for students with no Level II or III behaviors • Tickets to be used in "CATS" program for exhibiting behaviors on school matrix • Reward Menu for cashing in tickets

(Continued)

Table 3.11 (Continued)

	Academic	Behavior
Cut-Point for Referral to Tier 2	• Students scoring below benchmark in reading or math on universal screening tools	• Students with 2–5 ODRs • Students identified at risk through SRSS
Implementation Fidelity	• Lesson plan checks • Three formal observations per year for new teachers • Two formal observations per year for veteran teachers • Data collection using E-Walk	• Lesson plan checks • Observations of all teachers • Benchmarks of Quality completed yearly • Data collection using E-Walk

Table 3.12 Referrals by Month

Month	ADDR* (05–06)	ADDR* (06–07)	ADDR* (07–08)
August	1.62	1.36	1.33
September	3.68	4.35	3.47
October	5.25	4.38	3.15
November	6.37	5.74	3.68
December	6.08	5.53	4.29
January	4.10	3.41	2.83
February	7.53	4.00	4.17
March	5.86	5.38	4.32
April	6.07	3.20	4.33
May	6.70	4.16	3.88
Average for Year	5.41	4.24	3.53

* Average Daily Discipline Referrals

Figure 3.2   Average Referrals per Day per Month

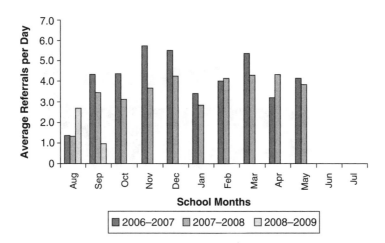

may indicate a need for staff development in making appropriate referrals or classroom management techniques. It could also indicate that expectations were not clearly taught to students at the beginning of the year. The leadership team decided to address both of these areas. Note that the referrals dropped significantly in September.

SUMMARY

This chapter has focused on development of a strong Tier 1 curriculum and support system. This tier will serve as the foundation for the entire RTI pyramid. As schools develop and implement a comprehensive RTI framework, they should incorporate academic and behavioral components into one seamless model. It should prove successful in teaching academics and managing behavior for approximately 80 percent of the student body. It should include a quality curriculum with both academic and behavioral components taught through differentiated instruction. Teachers should use formative and summative data to adjust instruction as needed. Comprehensive behavioral plans should be developed for both school-wide and classroom expectations. Universal screening should be used to identify which students need additional supports in Tiers 2 and 3. Attending to all these elements will provide a unified approach designed to maximize the potential for making all students successful learners.

Providing Targeted Supports Through Tier 2

Early intervention is considered to be one of the primary strengths of the RTI process. Because RTI provides a continuum of increasingly intensive interventions, student deficits can be addressed quickly and effectively. Interventions are designed to target specific academic and behavioral needs and to be feasible for implementation through general education. Frequent progress monitoring assists teachers and teams in making informed decisions to maximize student outcomes.

A large body of research has documented the benefits of providing early intervention to students at risk for school failure. For example, Vellutino and colleagues found that intensive reading interventions provided in kindergarten often reduced or eliminated the need for interventions in later grades (Vellutino, Scanlon, Small, & Fanuele, 2006). Behaviorally, proactive interventions provide significant improvements in student performance (Horner & Sugai, 2000). In the RTI model, these targeted interventions are provided in Tier 2. This level of support, considered necessary for 10–20 percent of the student population (Stewart et al., 2007), will be the focus of this chapter.

TIER 2 STRUCTURE AND TRAINING

The structure for Tier 2 support in an academic framework can take the form of Standard Protocol interventions and/or Problem-Solving team interventions, as discussed in Chapter 1. The most significant differences between these models are related to how decisions are made and how interventions are decided upon. Each has its own benefits and drawbacks. When using Standard Protocol interventions, all students with similar deficits receive the same interventions. This greatly improves fidelity because it limits the number of strategies in which the teacher or tutor must be trained. By contrast the Problem-Solving model requires that teams must have access to and training in a large number of interventions. Although this increases the likelihood that an intervention will be appropriate for the student, it may decrease the teacher's level of proficiency in the strategies. In both models interventions must be research-based and specific to the students' needs. These interventions may involve purchased programs and/or cognitive learning strategies appropriate across grade levels and content areas. Several resources for research-based academic strategies are given in Table 4.1.

In behavioral models both Standard Protocol and Problem-Solving teams may be used. Standard Protocol interventions may be established in the school based on the most common student needs. For example, a Behavior Education Program may be established in the school to address the common behavioral problems exhibited by students who don't respond to Tier 1 support alone. Schools may also put into place a standard intervention for students who have experienced a significant loss. Rainbows International, discussed later in this chapter, is a source for one such

Table 4.1   Resources for Research-Based Academic Strategies

- What Works Clearinghouse through the Institute for Education Sciences
  http://ies.ed.gov/ncee/wwc
- Florida Center for Reading Research
  www.fcrr.org/FCRRReports
- Institute for the Development of Educational Achievement
  www.reading.uoregon.edu
- The Access Center
  www.k8accesscenter.org
- Focus on Effectiveness
  www.netc.org/focus/strategies/
- Best Evidence Encyclopedia
  www.bestevidence.org/
- What Works Clearinghouse
  http://ies.ed.gov/ncee/wwc/
- Promising Practices Network
  www.promisingpractices.net/default.asp
- Promising Practices Network: Programs that Work
  www.promisingpractices.net/programs.asp
- Intervention Central
  www.interventioncentral.org/

intervention. In addition, schools may establish a peer mediation program in which students trained as mediators work to resolve conflicts between their peers. In each of these examples, interventions are preestablished and students are assigned as the need arises. Standard Protocol interventions can efficiently address the needs of most students in Tier 2, thereby reducing the time needed for problem-solving meetings on individual students (Crone et al., 2004).

When using Standard Protocol interventions, whether geared toward academic or behavior deficits, there should be a person or team designated to monitor student progress through data analysis, observations, and discussions with teachers. This may be the job of the data team discussed earlier. However, it can also be accomplished by an individual designated specifically for this purpose. In some schools a literacy facilitator or instructional coach is responsible for monitoring student progress with Tier 2 Standard Protocol reading and math interventions. A behavioral coordinator may also be designated for monitoring students' performance in behavioral interventions. The coordinator should meet with the students' teachers to discuss progress and make determinations for future instruction and support.

In addition to these Standard Protocol interventions, Problem-Solving teams are used to design effective behavioral interventions and support plans for individual students whose needs are not met by standard strategies. As stated earlier, Standard Protocol interventions are designed to address the most common deficits in the school. Some students may need interventions that are different from those that are preestablished. As schools begin Tier 2 development, the leadership team should lay the foundation for this process by establishing a support structure made up of multiple intervention teams. If possible, the membership of these teams should be different from the leadership and data teams used in Tier 1. Intervention teams will meet frequently to design appropriate behavior plans, closely monitor the students' response, and adjust instruction and supports as needed. In order to avoid overload and burnout of team members, schools should establish a number of intervention teams who will manage the supports for two to three students. Often schools develop a core team who will plan for multiple students and then add team members who are directly linked to each student being served. Core team membership may include the school counselor, behavior specialist, school psychologist, an administrator, social worker, and other persons with knowledge of behavioral interventions and programming. One person should be designated as case manager for each team. Each student's parents, teacher(s), and other individuals with specific knowledge about the student would be added.

Staff development for core team members is critical to the success of the intervention plan. Team members should represent several disciplines and have expertise in multiple areas. All should be well trained in the Problem-Solving process as outlined below, the principles of positive behavior supports, and using data for instructional decision making. One or more members should have knowledge of multiple interventions for a variety of behavior patterns and functions. In addition, at least one member must have a thorough understanding of functional behavioral assessment.

TIER 2 BEHAVIORAL PROCESS

Define the Problem

When a student is identified for Tier 2 support through a Problem-Solving approach, an intervention team as described above (also called student support or assistance team) should be formed. This team will analyze existing information about the student and collect additional information and data necessary to develop an appropriate intervention plan. They should begin by examining current student data and information, such as office discipline referrals, anecdotal records of problem behavior, academic functioning, school history, and family/social history in order to get a clear picture of the student's strengths, weaknesses, and any factors that could be contributing to his behavior. Teams should pay particular attention to factors such as how long the behavior has occurred and whether or not behavior problems seen at school also occur in community and home settings.

They should keep a running record of the student's behavior throughout the day. This will enable the team to look for patterns of behavior, such as the settings and time frame of occurrences, increases in problems before or after weekends and school breaks, or increases in problems that occur when the student is interacting with one person or a group, whether peer or adult. For example, some students have difficulty relating to women or may have a conflict with one particular teacher. Some may have more behavior problems in the afternoon than in the morning. These patterns may not be apparent to individual teachers, but become evident when documented and analyzed as part of the "big picture" of overall behavior occurrences.

Teams should pay particular attention to antecedent events. These are events that occur prior to the behavior and lead to or trigger the behavior. Antecedents may or may not take place immediately before a behavior incident. For example, a conflict on the school bus may be a trigger for a student's outburst at his teacher later in the day. For that reason it is important to explore and document the student's activities throughout the day.

The team should explicitly define and describe the problem behaviors and acceptable compliance in observable and measurable terms. For example, Jason is frequently out of his seat. In defining the behavior, the team will determine exactly what is meant by out-of-seat: losing contact with seat and standing when expected to sit (Fairbanks et al., 2007). This definition is both observable (the teacher can easily see if Jason is out of his seat) and measurable (the teacher can count the number of times he is out of his seat). In some instances the team may also need to define compliance: remaining in the seat unless directed otherwise. In contrast, saying that Jason is "wandering around" is not well defined and, therefore, is difficult to observe and measure.

Once the behavior is defined, the team should determine the baseline frequency of the problem behavior through interval recording. Baseline data indicates how often the behavior occurs at any given time. Interval recording involves documenting the number of times a behavior occurs in a specified interval or time frame. For example, at the request of the team, Jason's teacher kept a record of his out-of-seat behavior for three consecutive days and found that he was out of his seat an average of twelve times in a thirty-minute class period. This baseline data tells the team where to begin when setting a goal. Without this information there is no way to determine when Jason has made progress.

Teachers sometimes express concern that data collection of this type is difficult to accomplish while they are teaching. However, there are many easy ways to collect data that do not involve carrying a clipboard or stopping instruction to record events. For example, a teacher may record the number of times an incident occurs by putting items such as paperclips in a pants or apron pocket. Every time the incident occurs, one paperclip is moved to a different pocket. This is done for a specified time period (e.g., thirty minutes). At the end of the instructional period, the teacher simply counts and records the number of paperclips in the second pocket.

As the behavior is defined and data is collected and analyzed, the team is essentially conducting a brief functional behavioral assessment (FBA) in order to determine why the problem behavior is occurring. A behavior's function is the purpose or need that is fulfilled when the behavior occurs. The team's task will be to determine what function the behavior serves and to devise a plan that will teach the student more appropriate ways to achieve his purpose. This can be accomplished through the observations and interviews described in this section. At this level of intervention, it is not always necessary to conduct a formal and in-depth assessment. Simply looking at settings, antecedents, consequences, time frame, and student response will often reveal possible reasons for behaviors. However, the decision of how much assessment is needed should always be based on the individual needs of the student. A brief functional behavioral assessment checklist that allows documentation of the factors described above is provided in Resource C.

The team should also carefully examine the student's academic skills. As discussed earlier, many students exhibit problem behaviors in order to avoid a task or event that they consider unpleasant. Some students in a behavior problem-solving process may already receive interventions for an academic deficit. If the student has academic deficits that have not been addressed, interventions should be implemented immediately and concurrently with behavioral interventions. Team members should carefully monitor the student's performance with both sets of interventions.

In many instances the team may need to identify a replacement behavior—something that is designed to achieve the same function for the child but is more appropriate for the situation. In the example above, Jason may need more physical activity than the class routine has provided. Being out of his seat provides him with needed physical activity. The behavior occurs because Jason's need to move is stronger than his aversion to whatever consequence he receives when he is out of his seat. A replacement behavior might be to allow Jason to move between two work areas in the room when cued by the teacher. This will allow movement but restricts it to appropriate times. The teacher would need to provide the cue frequently enough to allow the movement to serve its purpose.

Plan the Intervention

After the team has developed a clear picture of the student's functioning and behavior, they will plan an intervention appropriate for the presenting problem. In Tier 2, interventions provide targeted support for small groups with similar problems or for individual students. They should be simple and easily implemented through general education. Schools should adhere to the philosophy of using the "weakest that works" (Waguespack et al., 2006; Yeaton & Sechrest, 1981). This will make it easy for teachers to implement the intervention and promote fading when the student has reached his goal.

Tier 2 interventions are designed to supplement rather than replace Tier 1 general instruction (McIntosh et al., 2006). Academic interventions, most often addressing deficits in reading and math, should be aligned with the core curriculum and provide more intensive instruction in the specific deficit skills (Vaughn & Roberts, 2007). Behavioral interventions should also align with Tier 1 social skills instruction and school-wide expectations while providing more intensive support and instruction to at-risk students (Horner, Hawken, & March, 2008). They should focus on behavioral instruction, specifically teaching expectations and appropriate replacement behaviors (Waguespack et al., 2006). Jason's teacher will use a form of self-monitoring to address the out-of-seat behavior. This intervention involves conferencing with the student to teach and clarify expectations, explaining the goal and replacement behaviors, and teaching the student to document his own behavior.

The team must also establish goals for reducing the problem behavior that specify the criteria for the desired and/or replacement behavior. When doing so it is important to develop both incremental and long-term goals. In our example the team's goal might be that Jason will be out of his seat no more than once in a thirty-minute period. While this goal is very appropriate, it may take many weeks to accomplish. If Jason receives no rewards until this goal is achieved, he will more than likely become frustrated and not work toward the goal. Recognizing Jason's need for frequent feedback, the team develops incremental goals. For example, the first goal is that Jason will be out-of-seat no more than eleven times in a thirty-minute period. When that goal is reached, Jason will work toward a goal of no more than ten out-of-seat occurrences in the thirty-minute period. This continual achievement and adjustment of the goal will provide ongoing feedback and encouragement for Jason, making attainment of the ultimate goal much more likely.

After identifying the intervention, the team must plan specific implementation components as outlined below.

1. Person(s) responsible for implementation and progress monitoring—dependent on the type of intervention. This usually involves the classroom teachers. However, as we will see later, another significant person may play a role in the intervention (see discussion of Check-in/Check-out). The team should also consider how the plan will be communicated to and possibly implemented by support personnel such as special area teachers (art, music, PE, etc.), bus drivers, clerical staff, cafeteria staff, and other adults who come in contact with the student during the day. Even if these persons are not actually implementing the interventions, it will be important for them to be aware of the student's plan so as not to inadvertently come in conflict with supports and interventions.

2. Time frame—This may include small group instruction (such as anger management group), continual implementation throughout the school day (such as behavior report card), or implementation in specific times and locations (check in with one person at beginning and end of school day).

3. Reward system—reinforcers that will be used and how/when they will be given

4. Progress monitoring tool—how the behavior change will be measured (such as percentage of possible points)

5. Frequency of progress monitoring—when and how often data will be collected

6. Frequency of progress review—how often the intervention team will meet to review data and adjust the instructional plan

7. Definition of responsiveness—how the team will determine that the student has responded appropriately to the intervention. This is most often, but not always, considered to be accomplishment of the goal.

As previously stated, Jason's team chooses a self-monitoring strategy to reduce his out-of-seat behavior. Teachers meet with him prior to beginning the strategy to discuss his baseline and expected outcome. They explain the strategy to him and explicitly teach their expectations, modeling how they want him to remain in his seat. They explain the replacement behavior, including limitations of when and how he can move between seats. They also demonstrate how his behavior will be monitored. Jason will begin each thirty-minute instructional period with twelve pieces of blue tape on his desk. Each time he gets out of his seat, he must remove one piece of tape. If he doesn't remove it himself, it will be removed by the teacher. Jason must have one piece of tape left at the end of the period in order to earn his reward. Jason chooses two reinforcers from the menu provided by the team. He understands that the reinforcer may be given immediately or he may receive a token to trade for it later in the class period. This strategy will be implemented during four instructional times throughout the day that were identified as being the most problematic. These times occur during language arts, math, social studies, and science classes.

Implement the Intervention

After developing the plan, it should be implemented as designed by the team. Measures should be put in place to assess fidelity of implementation. This may include observations, teacher self-checks, and student self-checks. Excellent strategies and programs, if implemented poorly, will produce poor results. Numerous issues related to fidelity of implementation were presented in Chapter 2. There are some fidelity issues that apply specifically to Tier 2. For example, the intervention must be carried out consistently by all individuals working with the student. Reinforcers must be appropriate for the student and given frequently enough to serve their purpose. Data collection must be consistent and should provide immediate feedback to the student, teacher, and parents.

Teams should also note how well the intervention is supported in non-treatment settings and generalize in everyday life (Sandomierski et al., 2007). For example, if a student receives instruction in a social skills group, interventions taught in the group should be ones that can be generalized and are effective in changing behavior in other settings. The strategies should also be taught and supported by the general education teachers and the resulting behavior improvements should be seen in the general education classroom. If the strategies result in improved behavior in the group, but have no effect on behavior in the classroom, they are considered ineffective (Rief, 2005).

Finally, it is important to document that the student receives the specified intervention as often as was prescribed. Student progress should be monitored and charted. This allows the team to quickly see student progress and make appropriate instructional decisions. In Chapter 2 several options were discussed for data management. Teams may also find that allowing students to chart their own data provides additional reinforcement and increases student motivation. This can be easily accomplished with previously discussed online tools, Microsoft Excel, or graph paper.

In our ongoing example, Jason's teachers implement the self-monitoring strategy during the specified classes. The school principal observes during one of the segments and finds that the teacher is using the strategy appropriately and consistently. Each teacher completes a checklist, documenting how well they have used the strategy and giving anecdotal information about Jason's response. In addition, each teacher collects daily data and either personally charts the information or allows Jason to chart his progress.

Evaluate the Student's Progress

Data-based decision making is critical to the success of the RTI model. Without it, even the best research-based interventions will prove ineffective (Nakasato, 2000). The team should reconvene every two to three weeks to discuss the student's progress. This will allow them to monitor the student's response closely and make adjustments in a timely manner.

Teams should carefully analyze and consider all data to determine if the intervention plan is successful. Changes should be made as called for by the data. The team will then determine the next steps for the student, whether to continue on the same track, change the plan, move forward to more intensive interventions, or discontinue and return the student to

Tier 1 supports. This process should be repeated as often as necessary to keep a successful plan in place for each student.

Teams should evaluate response based on whether or not the student meets the goals set by the intervention team, both incremental and long term. In our earlier example, Jason's long-term goal was one out-of-seat occurrence in a thirty-minute period. For several weeks Jason showed continual progress toward his goal. In Figure 4.1 we see that Jason obtained his goal after fourteen weeks of intervention.

Students who continue to exhibit significant behavioral problems, receive six or more ODRs, or whose behavior intensifies should be given more intensive assessment to determine the function of the behavior and to aid in development of a more appropriate intervention plan, perhaps implemented through Tier 3 intensive supports (Sugai, Horner, Dunlap, et al., 2000). This assessment and intervention process will be discussed in Chapter 5.

Teams may use criteria for determining responsiveness other than those listed above. For example, in a study of the effectiveness of the Behavior Education Program, the team defined and assessed unresponsiveness rather then responsiveness. They determined that students would be considered unresponsive if there was little change in rates of problem behavior, increasing trends in problem behavior, or continuation of serious disruptive behavior (Fairbanks et al., 2007). In some way the intervention team should specify the definition of responsiveness as part of the plan development and then carefully analyze all available information to determine if the student has met response criteria.

Figure 4.1   Average Referrals per Day per Month

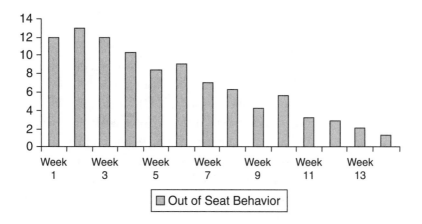

Research-Based Interventions for Addressing Problem Behaviors

When developing intervention plans, teams should choose explicit, well-designed interventions that target the function of the misbehavior. These interventions should be instructional and designed to teach appropriate expectations. They should be continuously available to students as needed in all settings. As outlined earlier, they should be easy to implement and require minimal effort from teachers (Horner et al., 2008).

Systematic targeted interventions have proven effective in reducing problem behaviors in most students. There are several factors that promote their success. First, they provide a focused structure for students. Throughout the day students receive consistent expectations, prompts, and feedback regarding their behavior. Secondly, the intervention plan usually links the student to at least one adult who will provide positive corrective feedback and support. The interventions can be applied in all settings that have adult supervision and by any number of different adults throughout the day. The student receives more adult attention for appropriate behaviors, thus reducing the need for inappropriate attention-seeking behaviors (Horner et al., 2008).

Proactive interventions essentially set the student up for success, reducing or eliminating antecedents that contribute to or cause the problem behaviors (Waguespack et al., 2006). Inappropriate behavior is less likely to be ignored or reinforced due to increased teacher understanding and attention to previous behavior patterns. The behavioral support is linked to academic performance and provides a home–school connection to increase parent contact. To promote long-term change, good intervention plans are designed to eventually become self-managing for the student, promoting responsibility and independence (Horner et al., 2008).

In Chapter 1 we discussed the need for the interventions to have a strong research base. OSEP's National Technical Assistance Center for School-Wide Positive Behavior Interventions and Supports promotes the use of interventions that have been researched through control-group studies as well as single-subject design and case studies. However, interventions with less comprehensive and intensive research documentation, such as case studies, should be carefully monitored (OSEP Center on Positive Behavioral Interventions and Supports, 2004; Sandomierski et al., 2007). Several interventions representing various levels of research will be discussed in this section. It is not meant to be an inclusive list, but is intended to provide guidance in the types of strategies proven to be effective as Tier 2 interventions. Additional behavioral research-based interventions may be found in the Matrix of Children's Evidence-Based

Practices. This document can be downloaded from www.systemsofcare .samhsa.gov/headermenus/docsHM/MatrixFINAL1.pdf.

Behavior Education Program or "Check-In, Check-Out"

One of the most commonly cited interventions in behavior research literature is the Behavior Education Program (BEP), also referred to as "Check-In, Check-Out" (CICO) or Check and Connect (Eber & Hawken, 2008). This Standard Protocol strategy uses daily behavior report cards to provide instruction, structure, and written feedback to students throughout the school day. Behavior report cards provide each student with a visual reminder of his or her personal goals and serve as a data collection tool. The strategy has a component to provide daily communication with parents. It can be used with individuals or groups of students who are exhibiting similar low-level behaviors (Fairbanks et al., 2007; Hawken & Horner, 2003; Todd, Campbell, Meyer, & Horner, 2008). As a standard protocol intervention, BEP procedures are established within the school and are available to any student whenever needed.

BEP contains a number of steps that students follow throughout each day. First the student meets with the designated BEP coordinator. At least one adult is assigned to be the BEP coordinator in the morning and afternoon. This may be a teacher, an administrator, a paraprofessional, a counselor, or even an office staff member. The person chosen for this responsibility should be someone who relates well and has a good rapport with students. This person will meet with students every morning, provide the daily behavior report card, help students get organized for the day, and provide encouragement and reminders of things that will make their day a success (Crone et al., 2004).

The school day is divided into intervals of time. This may be full class periods in a middle and high school, although class periods can be subdivided for students who need more frequent feedback. In elementary school teachers may divide the day by time periods (e.g., thirty minutes each) or class periods (e.g., reading, math, etc.). After each interval, the student presents the behavior report card to the teacher and is awarded points based on compliance with identified rules during the interval. At the end of the day, the student checks out with the BEP coordinator and receives some form of daily reinforcer in exchange for the points he has earned. Communication is sent home to the parent regarding the child's performance for that day. Students get their home communication signed and return it to the BEP coordinator the following morning (Crone et al., 2004; Todd et al., 2008).

In one study BEP was used with ten students in a second-grade classroom. BEP methods were similar to those described above, but were designed for use with just one class rather than an entire school. Office discipline referrals decreased from 0.85 per day to 0.41 per day within seven months of implementation. The interventions reduced problem behaviors by at least 38 percent. It was found to be highly successful with students exhibiting attention-seeking behaviors (Fairbanks et al., 2007). Two classroom teachers and the school counselor developed and implemented the program with minimal researcher input. They reported that it was easy to implement and improved the overall climate of the classroom. Students reported it as a positive experience as well (Fairbanks et al., 2007).

A similar study measured a BEP's effect on four students in kindergarten through fourth grade. These students averaged a 17.5 percent reduction from mean baseline to mean BEP levels. As in the previously mentioned study, school personnel were able to easily implement the intervention using resources that were already available. Data was reviewed for each student every two weeks and adjustments were made as needed (Todd et al., 2008).

This study also collected extensive data as evidence of program fidelity and feasibility. The researchers used a questionnaire and checklist to determine that BEP contained high social validation, which is the extent to which a program or strategy is perceived as effective and doable by the staff. Direct observation was conducted and verified that the problem behavior was reduced in the monitored academic period. ODR data showed that the positive effects were consistent across the school day (Todd et al., 2008).

BEP can serve as an effective Tier 2 intervention for students in all grades who exhibit attention-seeking behaviors. It can be adapted for students who are not seeking attention or who find adult attention aversive. It can also be modified for use as a Tier 3 intervention. It is recommended that the program serve fifteen to twenty students in a typical elementary school and no more than thirty students in a middle school (Crone et al., 2004).

The steps for typical BEP implementation are presented in Table 4.2. Additional information and resources can be found at www.ed.utah.edu/~hawken_l/bepresource.htm. This site, developed by Dr. Leanne Hawken, contains examples of daily behavior report cards, BEP forms, and a graphing program to chart student daily response. Another excellent resource that provides a full description of the process is a book titled *Responding to Problem Behavior in Schools* by Crone et al. (2004). This publication provides step-by-step instructions and forms that may be used by the purchaser of the book.

Table 4.2   Steps for Check-Behavior Education Program

1. Student meets with BEP coordinator in the morning. The previous day's parent letter is returned, signed by the parent.
2. Student receives daily Behavior Report Card (BRC).
3. BRC is taken to each class throughout the day.
4. At specified times, the student presents his BRC to the designated person in each class. This person awards points based on compliance during that time period.
5. Student meets with BEP coordinator.
6. Daily points are reviewed with student.
7. Parent communication form is sent home.

FIRST STEP TO SUCCESS

Another heavily researched targeted intervention program is First Step to Success (Carter & Horner, 2007; Todd et al., 2008). This program is a targeted intervention designed for students in kindergarten through second grade who are at risk for developing behavioral problems. The program is initially implemented by a trained coach who works with the teacher and parent to learn essential program components. The coach teaches the student to discriminate between appropriate and inappropriate behavior through a series of activities. Once the student is able to consistently demonstrate appropriate behaviors, the teacher takes over the program and continues classroom implementation. The teacher fades reinforcement from the frequent tangible rewards (food, stickers, etc.) used early in the process to intermittent natural consequences (verbal praise, good grades) that the student will experience in the natural setting. At the same time, parents receive training in setting limits, defining expectations, and supporting appropriate behaviors (Carter & Horner, 2007).

First Step to Success has strong empirical data documenting effectiveness in improving behavior and social skills of young children (Epstein & Walker, 2002; Lien-Thorne & Kamps, 2005). Those implementing the program have described it as easy to use, effective in teaching appropriate behavior, and effective in improving students' peer relations. It is a manualized program, meaning that it is explicitly described in implementation materials. It does, however, require that a consultant coach be trained in the process (Carter & Horner, 2007). Materials are available from Sopris West at www.sopriswest.com.

Responsibility Strategies

One key outcome associated with a behavioral RTI framework is having students increase independence and ownership of their behavior. Many students benefit from explicit instruction in strategies to increase student responsibility. Responsibility Strategy instruction was found to decrease disruptive behavior in high school students by as much as 34 percent and in middle school students by 30 percent (Marzano et al., 2003). This type of instruction is effective in improving academic performance, increasing classroom participation, and reducing behavioral problems. Two types of responsibility strategies that are the most effective are self-monitoring strategies and cognitively based strategies (Marzano et al., 2003).

Self-Monitoring Strategies

A direct link between academic engaged time (time on task) and learning is widely accepted and research supported (Cancelli, Harris, Friedman, & Yoshida, 1993; Rock, 2005; Stahr, Cushing, Lane, & Fox, 2006). Increasing engaged time involves a number of instructional factors including teaching style and differentiation of instruction (Rock, 2005). However, self-monitoring strategies have also proven very successful in increasing engagement (Marzano et al., 2003) as well as decreasing disruption and enhancing academic skills (Carr & Punzo, 1993) in students in Grades K–12. Self-monitoring strategies teach students to observe and record their own behavior, compare it with predetermined criteria, and reinforce their performance with established rewards (Marzano et al., 2003; Mather & Goldstein, 2008). These strategies have been found to be more effective with students with emotional behavior disorders than strategies controlled by the teacher (McQuillian & DuPaul, 1996). They have also been proven effective in increasing on-task behavior (Reid, Trout, & Schartz, 2005) and improving written expression skills (Reid & Lienemann, 2006) of students with attention deficit hyperactivity disorder (ADHD).

In a typical self-monitoring strategy, the student and teacher identify one to three behaviors that will be monitored. These may include behaviors such as work completion, talking out, or remaining in seat. The student is given a rubric or rating scale indicating expectations for behaviors to be perfomed (Harlacher, Roberts, & Merrell, 2006). The student then monitors her own performance, determining the amount of work completed or the accuracy of her work. She may then graph her performance. Self-monitoring strategies are often paired with reinforcement from the teacher (Reid et al., 2005).

Self-management is a form of self-monitoring in which the student compares her self-monitoring data with that collected by the teacher (Reid et al., 2005). At specified times or when given a signal, the student and the teacher rate the student's behavior on separate forms. After several documentation periods, the ratings are compared and the student receives points for each interval when her rating matched that of the teacher. Eventually, the teacher fades her rating, leaving the student to independent evaluation (Harlacher et al., 2006). This added component improves the student's accuracy and helps to teach appropriate expectations to the student.

Self-monitoring strategies may be divided into two categories: self-monitoring of attention (SMA) and self-monitoring of performance (SMP; Reid et al., 2005; Rock, 2005). SMA involves giving the student a cue to self-assess whether or not he is paying attention. The student then records his performance. SMP requires students to complete a task and then evaluate the completion or accuracy of their work. Both are used to increase engagement and accuracy of work (Reid et al., 2005).

Patton, Jolivette, and Ramsey (2006) identified five essential steps in developing a self-monitoring behavioral plan.

1. Identify and operationally define the behavior to be changed.
2. Determine the criteria for mastery, using baseline data.
3. Discuss appropriate and inappropriate behaviors with the student and reasons for the self-management plan.
4. Introduce the system for self-management.
5. Provide guided practice (Patton et al, 2006, pp. 15–16).

There are many variations of self-monitoring strategies in the literature. After receiving basic training in the process, intervention teams may also develop child-specific programs following the previous guidelines.

The following is a brief example of self-management strategy used with a fourth-grade student:

Katelyn is frequently off task. Her teacher, Ms. Hopkins, decides to use self-management to increase her on-task behavior, which she defines as participating in class and completing work on time as directed. Ms. Hopkins keeps a record of Katelyn's off-task behavior during independent practice activities in math class for three consecutive days. She does this by observing Katelyn's behavior at five-minute intervals for a total of thirty minutes each day and recording if Katelyn is on-task or off-task. Ms. Hopkins finds that Katelyn is off-task an average of 40 percent of the time.

She discusses her observation with Katelyn, including possible reasons that Katelyn is off-task. The reasons include distractions from friends and feeling hungry. Ms. Hopkins describes to Katelyn what it means to be on-task. She allows Katelyn to choose another area of the classroom where she will sit during math so as not to be distracted by her friends. Katelyn understands that she can move back to her seat near her friends when she has finished her math assignment. Ms. Hopkins then tells Katelyn that she will walk by her desk and tap her on the shoulder every five minutes during math. That is Katelyn's cue to observe her own behavior to determine if she is on-task. If so, she can place a checkmark on the behavior form taped to her desk. Ms. Hopkins will also record her behavior at that time. After class Katelyn and Ms. Hopkins will compare their observations. If they are in agreement and Katelyn was on task on four of six observations, she will earn a reward, which can include a snack.

After Katelyn has received all directions, Ms. Hopkins practices the strategy with her for ten minutes. They then agree that the strategy will begin the following day.

Interventions such as these can also be used with various technology devices such as tape recordings of "beeps" for attention signals, timers, or pagers set to vibrate at specific intervals. As students reach their goals, they should be rewarded and have new goals set (Mather & Goldstein, 2008). Increasing incremental goals will eventually lead students to the targeted behavior.

Cognitively Based Strategies

Many students engage in misbehavior because they react to problems rather than thinking through consequences (Marzano et al., 2003). Although it is assumed that thinking through and making appropriate choices is part of maturation and that students will acquire skills in this area, many students do not do so without assistance. This is related to a number of factors, including the students' self-perceptions and attitudes, the attitudes held by their peers, and their academic achievement (Ciechalski & Schmidt, 1995). For these children explicit instruction designed to teach them how to think through situations and make appropriate choices is essential.

Cognitively Based Strategies are used for improving behavior and academic performance. A summary of research found that students who received cognitive-based strategy instruction experienced a 28 percent decrease in disruptive behavior (Marzano et al., 2003). These strategies are designed to change the way students think about themselves, their environment, and their own behavior (Mather & Goldstein, 2008). Social skills training is one type of cognitive strategy used for behavioral improvement. Social skills training occurs when students are given direct instruction in how to handle social situations in the classroom (Eber & Hawken, 2008; Marzano et al., 2003; Todd et al., 2008). This sometimes occurs in small-group instruction through counseling programs. The behaviors are then generalized to the classroom where students are supported in using the strategies they've learned. Topics commonly taught include developing active listening skills, respecting personal space, reading social signals, and managing anger (Rief, 2005).

Self-Determination

The ability to choose your own outcomes can be a powerful incentive for behavioral change (Janney & Snell, 2008; Kern et al., 1998). Self-determination and choice-making can lead to improved social behavior, increased task performance, and reduced problem behaviors (Dunlap et al., 1994). Researchers have found that behavior problems decrease and on-task behaviors increase when students are given a choice of assignments or options as to the order of assignment completion (Dunlap, Kern-Dunlap, Clarke, & Robbins, 1991; Seybert, Dunlap, & Ferro, 1996). Students show positive response to choices as simple as which desk they prefer to sit in to complete an assignment.

Self-determination is multifaceted. In order to make appropriate choices for themselves, students must first be able to understand their own strengths, weaknesses, and preferences. They must also be able to identify and set personal goals, and take action to achieve those goals. They must then evaluate the outcomes of their actions and adjust their plans or goals accordingly (Martin & Marshall, 1996, as cited in Meyers & Eisenman, 2005). Many students do not acquire these skills through everyday occurrences and need direct instruction in one or more of these areas. This may be done through individual or small-group training.

In addition, students may be given opportunities to have control over their circumstances through active involvement in the decision-making process of developing their behavior intervention plan, including setting goals and selecting reinforcers. In classroom behavior plans, self-determination can be accomplished by teaching students effective skills for problem solving and decision making in social situations (Wehmeyer, Baker, Blumberg, & Harrison, 2004).

There are many published programs available for teaching self-determination. One such program is *Steps to Self-Determination: A Curriculum to Help Adolescents Learn to Achieve Their Goals* (Hoffman & Field, 2005). This program helps students identify their strengths, weaknesses, needs, and preferences; develop decision-making skills; set goals; anticipate consequences; and develop negotiation skills. It also contains a Self-Determination Knowledge Scale to track student progress.

Additionally, the Alaska Department of Education has a Self-Determination Toolkit containing assessment tools, lesson plans, and a video appropriate for teaching these skills. Although the kit was specifically designed for high school students with disabilities, the lesson plans are appropriate for younger students and for students of all ages without disabilities. Lesson topics include communication styles, listening skills, assertiveness skills, negotiating, and handling feedback. Each lesson plan includes student handouts. The toolkit is available free of charge from www.alaskachd.org/toolkit.

Rainbows International

"Rainbows" is a grief support program for students ages 3 through adult. It is a twelve-week curriculum that includes activities, discussion, and reflections to help students accept loss, whether from death of a family member, divorce, or other separation. Small-group sessions are led by trained facilitators who may be teachers, paraprofessionals, clerical staff, or community volunteers. Training sessions are held throughout the country several times each year. Students may repeat the cycle as often as they desire. The session cycle ends with a "Celebrate Me" day (Rainbows International, 2008). Information can be obtained at www.rainbows.org.

Other Strategies

A variety of additional strategies are recommended for Tier 2 interventions throughout the literature on School-Wide Positive Behavior Interventions and Supports (SWPBIS) and behavior management in general. These strategies may have somewhat less research to support them, but are considered appropriate for use as targeted interventions. In addition, many programs, both purchased and locally developed, are implemented through the guidance and counseling offices of most schools. These may include anger management groups and conflict resolution training.

PROGRESS MONITORING FOR TIER 2

A major component of Tier 2 is increased frequency of progress monitoring. Tier 1 universal screening assesses all students in the school periodically throughout the school year. In Tier 2 progress is monitored more frequently, sometimes as often as weekly or daily. This allows intervention teams to make appropriate decisions early in the intervention process, thus maximizing the effect of the intervention (Chafouleas et al., 2007). Academic progress is measured using curriculum-based measurement (CBM) tools. CBM uses quick assessments or probes that measure small increments of progress on basic skills. A commonly used CBM tool for elementary reading is the Dynamic Indicators of Basic Early Literacy Skills (DIBELS).

Behavioral assessment may be accomplished through the use of multiple types of assessments. Schools should first follow up on the universal screening tool that was used to identify the student for Tier 2 interventions. For example, if a student was identified using ODRs, the intervention team should continue to monitor that data during Tier 2 interventions. With adequate response the team should see a reduction from the initial occurrences.

In addition, the team may monitor externalizing problem behaviors through interval recording as illustrated in our earlier examples in which the teacher counted the number of occurrences in a given time period (Janney & Snell, 2008). Initially, this should be done daily, and can be faded to weekly monitoring after the behavior has decreased significantly. The data should be graphed for later analysis. It is also a good idea to keep anecdotal records of unusual or significant factors that may have affected the behavior, including student absences, altercations, or change in routine (Janney & Snell, 2008). Teams may use a simple documentation chart individualized for the student in order to record the data. An example is shown in Table 4.3. A blank form for this purpose is available in Resource B.

Many behavioral interventions have progress monitoring built into the program. For example, the Behavior Education Program described earlier involves keeping a daily behavior report card that documents the student's performance throughout the day. By recording this performance in an ongoing record or chart, the intervention team can easily monitor responsiveness as evidenced by daily data.

Finally, teams should gather data on occurrence of the replacement behavior. This may be charted on the same graph as the interval recording of problem behavior for comparison purposes. As the problem behavior decreases, teams should expect to see the replacement behavior being used more frequently (Janney & Snell, 2008).

Table 4.3   Simple Data Collection Form

Student name: __James_____ Date: __10/8/08_____

Observer: __Cathy Cauffman_____

Data collection method: __Moved rubberbands from one arm to another for each incident

_____

_____

Time Frame	10:10– 10:20	10:20– 10:30	10:30– 10:40	10:40– 10:50	10:50– 11:00
Activity	Math teacher directed instruction	Math teacher directed instruction	Math guided practice	Math independent practice	Math independent game
Behavior: hitting other students	4	6	3	5	0

Anecdotal information: _____

Teams may collect other data as indicated by the student's specific problem. Data collection may include overall review of school records, number of timeouts and suspensions, grade point average, and number of tardies/absences (Lane, Parks, et al., 2007). In addition, they may choose to use a behavioral checklist such as the Systematic Screening for Behavior Disorders (SSBD) discussed in Chapter 3 (H. Walker & Severson, 1992). Completion of checklists, direct observation, and anecdotal information from teachers and parents may be especially important in monitoring the progress of students with internalizing behaviors.

Teams must analyze data to determine whether or not the student has shown appropriate response to the intervention. When data reveals a significant decrease in problem behaviors and mastery of long-term goals, supports should be faded to determine if the student could be successful with Tier 1 support alone. When data reveal no significant change, teams should explore the appropriate next steps for the student. It is always important to keep in mind that behavior change is often a very slow process. In general, the longer a behavior problem has existed, the longer it will take to extinguish it (B. Walker et al., 2005). Consistent application of interventions over an extended period of time proves to be most effective.

Students who do not show adequate response to Tier 2 interventions may need further assessment through the use of a Functional Behavioral Assessment process. This type of assessment is more intensive than those discussed previously and serves the purpose of identifying antecedents and consequences that may be causing the behavior (Chafouleas et al., 2007). Functional Behavioral Assessment is most often used with students who are being considered for or are receiving interventions in Tier 3. The process will be discussed at length in Chapter 5.

Fidelity of Implementation

It is imperative to evaluate fidelity of implementation of Tier 2 interventions before making a determination as to whether or not students have responded adequately. Fidelity includes discerning if the intervention was implemented as designed as well as if the intervention generalized to non-treatment settings (Sandomierski et al., 2007). In a survey of PBIS implementation in all fifty states, Killu and colleagues (2006) found that implementation fidelity was the least frequently addressed issue in PBIS materials. In my experience it is the component of both academic and behavioral RTI frameworks that is most likely to be overlooked. However, ensuring the extent to which Tier 1 and Tier 2 interventions have been implemented with fidelity and integrity to the original design is essential in determining if students have received adequate instruction.

Teams should first determine if the intervention has been delivered as often as prescribed. This is often revealed through careful examination of daily student data. For example, an interventionist providing reading or math instruction may be asked to record each occurrence of the instruction. Similarly, daily behavior report cards will document student absences and days on which the intervention was used.

In Chapter 2 we discussed the use of the School-Wide Evaluation Tool (SET) and the Benchmarks of Quality (BoQ) to evaluate overall school-wide implementation of the process and universal supports. In Tier 2 checklists and observations are the most common forms of assessment for ensuring fidelity (Fairbanks et, al., 2007). For example, schools may develop a fidelity checklist that outlines the critical features of the intervention being used. This checklist can be used by an administrator, school counselor, or peer teacher to evaluate the instructor's accuracy in teaching the strategy. The percentage for implementation fidelity may be calculated by dividing the number of components implemented by the number not implemented and multiplying by 100 percent (Fairbanks et al., 2007). As mentioned above, intervention teams should also maintain records of the frequency of implementation. For example, if a teacher was absent for two days and the substitute teacher did not implement a prescribed behavioral intervention, the student outcome would most likely be adversely affected. That information would be very important in the decision-making process.

In choosing intervention strategies, teams should always consider contextual fit. This indicates whether or not the intervention is consistent with the resources, skills, and values of the staff and the administrative support available to them (Todd et al., 2008). Interventions that lack contextual fit will be rejected by the staff and not implemented with fidelity. The Self-Assessment of Contextual Fit in Schools (Horner, Salantine, & Albin, 2003) is a sixteen-item checklist designed to assess this aspect of instructional fidelity (Todd et al., 2008).

Another tool that can prove very useful is the Checklist for Individual Student Systems available at www.pbis.org. This checklist helps schools and leadership teams determine the percentage of key features that are in place in the school. It also helps team members rank priorities for future planning.

CASE STUDY OF TIER 2 INTERVENTION PLAN

Jayda is a seventh-grade student identified by her teacher as having frequent verbal outbursts. Specifically, Jayda yells out answers to questions before being called on and argues when given assignments that she doesn't like. These behaviors occur occasionally throughout the school day, but most often during the afternoon. These behaviors have worsened over the past few weeks, prompting Jayda's math teacher, Mr. Baines, to bring the matter to the school's Problem-Solving team, which includes the school counselor, the behavior specialist, all of Jayda's teachers, and her parents. The following is a summary of the team's application of RTI elements and the Problem-Solving cycle.

Quality of Tier 1 instruction: Mr. Baines has developed a generally effective behavior management plan in his classroom. Students were taught behavioral expectations each day during the first few weeks of school. Direct teaching of expectations was not faded until the class followed the rules on a consistent basis. Rules and consequences for breaking them are posted in the classroom. There are five rules all stated in a positive manner. They are: (1) Bring book and materials to class, (2) Raise your hand before speaking, (3) Respect other people and their property, (4) Follow instructions the first time they are given, and (5) Complete all assignments as directed. Mr. Baines also has a small bulletin board in the classroom dedicated to social skills development and behavioral expectations. Each week he teaches one or more ten-minute lessons on appropriate social skills. A reward system is in effect in which students earn a token each day for rule compliance. In addition, all students and their parents signed a behavior contract at the beginning of the school year. Mr. Baines has referred no students to the office this school year.

Tier 2 Intervention Plan

Define the problem:

- Verbal outbursts—defined as any verbal communication that interrupts the teacher or other person without the student being called on (Fairbanks et al., 2007)
- Compliance—defined as accepting assignments from teacher without verbal or physical opposition.
- External contributing factors—Jayda has a history of excessive talking documented by previous teachers. Her parents report behaviors at home that are similar to those seen in the classroom. She is the second of four children. She often aggressively competes for her parents' attention.
- Data analysis—before the initial meeting, the school counselor observed Jayda for thirty minutes during a seventy-minute math block. During the observation Jayda exhibited twelve verbal outbursts and two acts of noncompliance. The team also reviewed Jayda's academic functioning. Her most recent standardized assessment scores place Jayda in the 75th percentile for math and

80th percentile for reading skills and comprehension. The team determines that, based on these scores, Jayda should be able to complete the assignments given to her.

Plan the intervention:

- Intervention—Daily Behavior Report Cards (Chafouleas et al., 2007; Crone et al., 2004)—This intervention is an adaptation of the Behavior Education Program that allows the concept to be used with an individual student. Jayda will check in with her homeroom teacher every morning. She will receive a Behavior Report Card to be completed by all her teachers throughout the day. The Behavior Report Card will provide a place for teachers to rate her behavior in each class. Items will specifically target verbal outbursts and compliance. Jayda will check out with her homeroom teacher in the afternoon. At that time she will receive feedback on her behavior and a note summarizing her progress for her parents.
- Person responsible for implementation and progress monitoring— classroom teachers and homeroom teacher. Jayda's parents agree to check the home report daily and follow through with praise and rewards at home.
- Time frame—daily for all segments.
- Goal—Initially, Jayda will receive a reward for earning 75 percent of all possible points. The goal will be increased in five-point increments as she meets the previous goal. Additionally, Jayda will receive verbal praise each time she earns a point.
- Reward system—Jayda chose to receive tokens that can be traded for supplies at the school store, for dance passes, or used for silent auctions.
- Progress monitoring tool—percentage of points earned.
- Frequency of progress monitoring—daily.
- Frequency of progress review—every three weeks.
- Definition of responsiveness—achievement of the long-term goal of 95–100 percent of all possible points for two consecutive weeks.

Implement the intervention:

- Mr. Baines and the school counselor met with Jayda to discuss the intervention. They discussed the problem behavior and reasons the behavior was not acceptable. They discussed and modeled the appropriate behavioral expectations. They also discussed her baseline data and the incremental goals they had set for her. Jayda was asked to choose one or two rewards, which are outlined above.

They then explained to Jayda the procedures for using the Behavior Report Card. Finally, they asked Jayda if she was willing to participate in the intervention plan. She agreed.

- Mr. Baines and the other teachers implemented the intervention as specified. The school counselor observed for fidelity of instruction in three classrooms during the first week. She found that the plan was being implemented consistently and appropriately.
- Jayda's parents checked the home report on a somewhat consistent basis. It was returned 80 percent of the time.

Evaluate the student's progress:

- Results of the intervention are illustrated in Figure 4.2. During the second week of implementation, Jayda earned 75 percent of her points on two days. During the third week, she earned 75 percent on four days.
- The goal will be raised to 80 percent for an additional three weeks. Progress will again be reviewed at that time.

Figure 4.2 Jayda's Behavior Chart

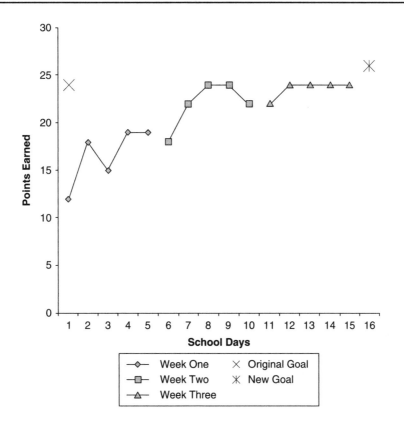

SUMMARY

Tier 2 support through RTI is an effective means of remediating both behavioral and academic deficits. Targeted interventions provide specific instruction and support for students at risk. These interventions may be standard protocols that are available to all students or individualized based on findings of the Problem-Solving team. These interventions should have an appropriate base of research to substantiate their effectiveness for the identified problems. Teams should monitor implementation fidelity to ensure that instruction is occurring as it should.

Ongoing progress monitoring provides intervention teams with objective data for instructional decision making. Teams must review student progress frequently and make adjustments to interventions in response to minute changes in student performance. A student's responsiveness should guide the team in determining the next steps for instruction and intervention.

With appropriate support most students who receive Tier 2 interventions should eventually be able to experience success with Tier 1 supports only. The goal of Tier 2 interventions is to provide support beyond that available to all students in order to teach specific skills students are lacking. This is true for both academic and behavioral interventions. When combined into a comprehensive RTI model, the intervention plan can address most student needs and provide supports designed to make the majority of students successful.

Delivering Intensive Individual Supports Through Tier 3

The RTI process is an excellent tool for providing appropriate instruction and interventions for all students within a school. Tiers 1 and 2, when implemented well, should provide effective instruction for approximately 95 percent of the student body. However, there is usually a small group of individuals for whom the universal and targeted interventions do not prove effective. Tier 3 is designed to provide intensive individualized supports for these students.

Although this group usually comprises only 1–5 percent of the student body, their supports and instruction require a large percentage of the school's resources. In many schools this group accounts for 40–50 percent of all problem behaviors in the school (Stewart et al., 2007). This chapter will focus on the assessment and supports that are most often necessary to provide effective instruction for these students.

IDENTIFICATION OF TIER 3 STUDENTS

After students have received appropriate small-group or individual targeted interventions through Tier 2 instruction, the intervention team must determine whether the student has made acceptable gains. As discussed in the previous chapter, various types of data are examined to evaluate each student's response. When Tier 2 strategies have proven unsuccessful, the student moves to Tier 3 to receive individualized planning, assessment, and supports.

In an academic RTI framework, students who progress to Tier 3 almost always do so by passing through Tiers 1 and 2. Lack of response and ongoing low achievement are used as evidence that a student needs more intensive support and, in some cases, as evidence that the student may have a Specific Learning Disability (L. S. Fuchs & Fuchs, 2007). Tier 2 nonresponders receive further evaluation and intensive individualized interventions provided in Tier 3.

This progression through Tiers 1 and 2 may not always occur in the behavioral framework. There are a variety of ways to identify students who need Tier 3 behavioral supports. One common cut-point involves the number of office discipline referrals (ODRs) received by a student during a school year. Students with six or more ODRs may need immediate access to this level of support (Fairbanks, Simonsen, & Sugai, 2008; McIntosh et al., 2006; Sugai, Sprague, et al., 2000). This may include students who are chronically disruptive, violent, or exhibiting self-destructive behaviors (Stewart et al., 2007).

Secondly, students who have significant risk factors for problem behavior may also require immediate access to Tier 3 interventions (Kern & Manz, 2004; Lane, Wehby, Robertson, & Rogers, 2007). As discussed in Chapter 3, these students may be detected through assessment procedures such as teacher referrals and checklists designed to identify the presence of risk factors. Students exhibiting significant risk factors may receive Tier 3 interventions as a preventive measure, even if no significant behavioral problems have previously occurred.

Today's students experience a wide range of environmental and familial situations that may cause these risk factors. For example, in 2005 18 percent of all children under the age of 18 lived in poverty. The highest rates of poverty were for African American (35 percent) and Hispanic (28 percent) children. Many of these children (54 percent) lived in single-parent homes where the mother was unemployed or underemployed (Forum on Child and Family Statistics [FCFS], 2007). Poor children, regardless of race or ethnicity, are more likely to experience development delays, drop out of school, and give birth as teenagers (Miranda, 1991, as cited in Payne, 2005). Children whose mothers have less than a high school education are less likely to be read to daily (FCFS, 2007) and often come to school lacking the skills they need to be successful academically and behaviorally (Payne, 2005). In 2005 7 percent of children living below the poverty level had serious emotional or behavioral difficulties, compared with 4 percent of children in nonpoor families (FCFS, 2007).

Another significant factor that places children at risk is the presence of parental abuse. Twenty percent of America's children live in families where at least one parent abuses alcohol. Alcohol is a significant factor in 81 percent of child abuse cases (Johnson, 2001, as cited in Marzano et al., 2003). In 2005 substantiated reports of child abuse or neglect involved 762,385 children (National Data Analysis System [NDAS], 2007).

There are numerous other factors that may place a student at risk for serious behavioral problems. These include early indicators such as premature birth, low birth weight, prenatal substance abuse, and birth injury. In addition, children who have experienced extended periods of isolation or deprivation may suffer long-term difficulties. Students who exhibit extreme social isolation should be considered for possible Tier 3 supports (Janney & Snell, 2008).

Finally, students with severe internalizing behaviors may also need immediate access to Tier 3 supports. This includes children with a variety of mood disorders. Depression affects about 8 percent of all adolescents in the United States (U.S. Department of Health and Human Services, as cited in Marzano et al., 2003). Mood disorders such as depression, dysthymia, and bipolar disorders are indicated in as many as 90 percent of children and adolescents who commit suicide (Child Trend Data Bank [CTDB], 2007).

As discussed previously, the use of ODRs as the primary universal screening tool fails to identify most students with risk factors and internalizing behaviors such as these. Students with high-risk factors, withdrawn behaviors, and/or self-destructive behaviors can be identified through checklists such as the SSBD or through identification by teachers, counselors, parents, or others (Stewart et al., 2007).

TIER 3 AND SPECIAL EDUCATION

There is a great deal of confusion among educators as to how special education fits into the RTI framework. This confusion often causes uncertainty as to whether or not a student may receive Tier 3 instruction and support. The confusion is justified in part because the decision of where special education fits into the pyramid is left to the discretion of each state department of education.

In general, Tier 3 should not be thought of as a label synonymous with any special program. Tier 3 supports are individualized and intensive. A student who is in need of this level of instructional intensity should receive that type of support. If a student is eligible for special education services, he may receive the support through special education. If he is not eligible, he may receive the support through general education. The bottom line is that the student needs intensive instruction and support.

Educators should think of the RTI pyramid as a system of increasingly intensive supports and progress monitoring. Students appropriate for Tier 1 are successful with instruction provided for all students within the school. Students in Tier 2 are in need of additional, more intensive targeted supports and progress monitoring. Students who are unsuccessful with Tier 2 supports need even more intensive instruction, supports, and progress monitoring provided through Tier 3.

From the standpoint of RTI theory and research, academic and behavioral interventions in Tier 3 may be provided through special education services or outside of special education. However, as stated earlier, the ultimate decision of how the two fit together lies with each state department of education. In some states Tier 3 involves only special education services. In others special education is considered to be outside of the RTI framework. In still others students who qualify for special education services receive their Tier 3 supports under the umbrella of special education; those who do not meet special education eligibility receive intensive services through general education. Every teacher and administrator should seek a clear understanding of their state's regulations and guidelines regarding this issue.

It is assumed that a student who is eligible for special education may need the type of intensive support provided in Tier 3. It should not be assumed that only students with disabilities will need this level of support. This should be given careful consideration as states and districts develop guidelines and regulations for RTI implementation.

One important point to remember is that students served in Tier 3 should not receive less intensive support than is provided in Tier 2. For example, a student who is unsuccessful with small-group targeted reading instruction in Tier 2 will need more intensive instruction in Tier 3. This student, if served through special education, may also need support in general education classrooms through inclusion in order to access the general curriculum. This balance of services and support are essential in providing appropriate instruction for all students.

PLANNING FOR TIER 3 STUDENTS

When students are identified as needing Tier 3 academic or behavioral supports, a comprehensive planning process should be put in place. In most cases an intensive support team should be formed. This team should include members from the Tier 2 team, such as parents, teachers, administrators, and behavioral specialists, but is usually expanded to include special education teachers if appropriate, mental health workers, social workers, school psychologists, therapists, and others with expertise in intensive assessment and interventions and knowledge about the student. Tier 3 teams should always reflect the needs of the child and family (Eber & Hawken, 2008). The team should meet frequently, in some cases as often as weekly, to develop intensive supports based on the student's identified needs.

Supports at this level are not always limited to school-based interventions. Due to the complexity of behaviors exhibited by these students, the Tier 3 intervention team must take into account external forces and contributing factors that may be causing many of the behavioral problems seen at school. Therefore, inclusion of representatives from community agencies may be essential in developing an effective intervention plan (Barnett et al., 2006).

ASSESSMENT

The Tier 3 process often begins with individualized assessment. When planning for academic interventions, this may involve a multidisciplinary educational evaluation for the purpose of answering questions raised during earlier intervention tiers (L. S. Fuchs & Fuchs, 2007). Assessment tools utilized in this process may include IQ tests, individual achievement tests, and teacher/parent checklists. The results are analyzed to determine the presence of a disabling condition and/or to document the need for specially designed individualized instruction.

In a behavioral framework, academic functioning levels should also be considered. If the student has deficits in reading or math, particularly, the intervention team should obtain academic assessment results and plan appropriate interventions. The team may also conduct functional record review, ecological interviews, and structured parent and teacher reports (Barnett et al., 2006).

However, the most common form of assessment used in Tier 3 behavioral planning is Functional Behavioral Assessment (FBA). Individualized Functional Behavior Assessments are essential in providing appropriate interventions to students with significant behavioral problems (Ingram, Lewis-Palmer, & Sugai, 2005). FBA is a process of gathering specific data to determine why a behavior occurs in a particular setting (Waguespack et al., 2006). FBA examines setting events and consequences that predict and maintain inappropriate behaviors. It involves the use of a variety of tools including both direct and indirect measures (Fairbanks et al., 2007).

Direct assessment involves observations of student behavior in a setting where the behavior most often occurs or is likely to occur (Waguespack et al., 2006). The observations are often completed by a psychologist, behavioral specialist, or special education teacher. Behavior occurrences are recorded and charted. Direct assessments may also involve the use of a standardized tool such as the Functional Assessment Observation Form (FAOF; O'Neill et al., 1997) or an Antecedent-Behavior-Consequence (ABC) checklist (Todd et al., 2008). Typical data includes antecedent events, settings, consequences, and other contributing factors. It is then analyzed in an effort to determine why the behavior is occurring and the factors that are maintaining the behavior.

Although they yield the most comprehensive data, direct assessments are often considered unfeasible in school settings. They require a great deal of time and resources that may not always be available. They also do not accurately identify significant behaviors that occur infrequently, such as possession of weapons or drugs and acts of violence or aggression (Waguespack et al., 2006).

Indirect assessments include tools such as structured interviews, checklists, questionnaires, and rating scales completed by the parent, teacher, or child (Janney & Snell, 2008). They are usually easy to complete, require less time than direct assessments, and provide information from a variety of sources. Examples of indirect measures found frequently in research and literature include the Functional Assessment Interview (FAI; O'Neill et al., 1997) and the Functional Assessment Checklist for Teachers and Staff (FACTS; March et al., 2000).

The usefulness of indirect assessments in providing valid and reliable data has been questioned. However, research supports the validity of many such tools. In one study, McIntosh and colleagues (2006) found that the reliability and validity of the FACTS was strong. They concluded that indirect assessment methods play an important role in FBA, despite the fact that they are less rigorous than direct assessments. They recommended that individuals using the tools receive training and ongoing support in order to maximize the reliability and validity (McIntosh et al., 2006). The FACTS is available from www.pbis.org.

In a similar study, Ellingson and colleagues (2000) determined that teachers were able to complete a structured behavioral questionnaire and provide reliable and valid information regarding antecedents and consequences, even when they had not received formal training in FBA. The researchers concluded that checklists may be as effective as interviews in providing this information (Ellingson et al., 2000). With limited training, teachers have been able to identify setting events and antecedents within classrooms and formulate hypothesis statements using these tools (Wright-Gallo, Higbee, Reagon, & Davey, 2006). While it is always important to include a variety of assessment tools in an FBA, these findings are important to schools in that indirect assessments may be considered a feasible supplement to direct methods.

FBA is a more extensive, structured, and formal process than the brief FBA discussed in Chapter 4. It should result in very specific outcomes. First, the team should develop an operational definition of the problem behavior that is both observable and measurable. Secondly, the team should identify the antecedent events that reliably predict the occurrence and nonoccurrence of the behavior. Finally, the team should identify a consequence or event that maintains the behavior (McIntosh, Borgmeier, et al., 2008). When these outcomes are accomplished, the results are then used to hypothesize the function of the behavior and develop a function-based support plan for the student. That support plan should include strategies to teach appropriate skills and to change the environment for the purpose of making the problem behavior no longer serve its function (McIntosh et al., 2006). We will take a closer look at each of these outcomes in order to fully understand the FBA process.

OUTCOMES OF FBA

Step 1: Establish an Operational Definition of the Problem Behavior

In conducting an FBA, the team should begin by defining the targeted behavior in observable and measurable terms. A baseline assessment of the frequency and duration of the behavior should be collected. Just as in Tier 2, baseline data will be used to establish the goal and monitor the student's progress toward that goal (Janney & Snell, 2008). It should be current and should be a direct measure of the identified behavior. To obtain baseline the observer provides specific data for at least three time intervals (class periods, days, etc.). All data is charted, and the median score is considered the baseline (Shores & Chester, 2008).

> EXAMPLE: Kayla hits adults and other students with her hands and other objects such as books. This behavior has occurred daily for three months. During the past three days, Kayla has engaged in this behavior eight, twelve, and nine times during the two-hour period after lunch. Baseline occurrence of the behavior is nine occurrences.

Step 2: Identify Antecedents

Antecedents describe what is occurring when the behavior is exhibited. They provide information regarding how the environment and behavior are related, and ultimately may lead to understanding the function of the behavior. To determine the antecedent for a specific behavior, we must learn what takes place just prior to and when the behavior occurs. For example, if a student has frequent outbursts when given a writing task, the antecedent is assignment of a writing task. The function of the behavior may be to avoid tasks that are perceived by the student to be too difficult or aversive. Common antecedents may include specific events (e.g., assignment of a particular task), people (e.g., specific teacher or all females), conditions (e.g., unstructured settings), and places (e.g., school cafeteria) that trigger certain behaviors (Janney & Snell, 2008).

Setting events are specific types of antecedents that exist within the person or the environment. They include biological, physical, or social incidents or circumstances that make it more likely that a behavior will occur (Janney & Snell, 2008). These may include physical symptoms such as pain or lack of sleep, social-emotional factors such as family discord, environmental factors such as arriving late to school, and learning and self-regulation factors such as distress over schedule changes (Crimmins, Farrell, Smith, & Bailey, 2007). For example, if a student has an argument with her mother before leaving for school, she may be more likely to react negatively when a seemingly minor incident happens later in the day. Likewise, if a student has not had sufficient sleep, he may become suddenly agitated at a simple request from his teacher later in the day. Often, setting events can only be identified through interviews with parents and others outside the school setting. The team should explore variables commonly referred to as Quality of Life Indicators. These include areas such as family life, the student's relationships with adults and peers within and outside the school setting, events and activities where the student experiences success within and outside the school, their interests and preferences, and opportunities to make age-appropriate choices. In talking with family members and others directly involved with the student, the team may be able to identify frequently occurring setting events that trigger both positive and negative behaviors. For example, a student may feel anger and bitterness about his parents' divorce. This may trigger certain behaviors after spending time with the noncustodial parent. As the team develops an intervention plan, it is important to understand this relationship and to know when these triggers are likely to occur.

Determining the relationship between the antecedent and the behavior is essential in developing appropriate intervention plans (Killu et al., 2006). It allows the team to eliminate or control variables in the environment in order to prevent or decrease problem behaviors. For example, if we know a student has difficulty in unstructured environments, we can limit these types of settings in his school day (Janney & Snell, 2008).

> EXAMPLE: After observing Kayla in her classroom and other settings around the school, the psychologist determines that the behavior occurs most often when Kayla is being ignored by other children. The antecedent seems to be a lack of attention from her peers. It may be that Kayla needs to be taught how to obtain her friends' attention in more positive ways.

Step 3: Identify a Consequence That Maintains the Behavior

It is also important for the team to determine the effect of consequences on the behavior. Consequence refers to any events, both natural and imposed, that occur after the behavior (Janney & Snell, 2008). Consequences serve the purpose of reinforcing and thus maintaining the behavior. Analysis of consequences helps to identify the function served by the behavior.

Many times consequences serve purposes that are different than we expect or anticipate. For example, negative attention from peers or adults can be quite rewarding to some students. If the function of the student's behavior is to seek attention, he or she may not care whether it is positive or negative attention. When the attention is gained, the behavior has served its function. Teams must keep this in mind as they analyze student behaviors and responses to consequences.

EXAMPLE: When Kayla hits other children, all attention becomes focused on her. Her peers often scold her and tell her that she is being mean. Her teacher stops instruction and reprimands her. She gains the attention that she wants, albeit in a negative manner. It doesn't matter to Kayla that she has gained negative attention. What matters is that she has gained attention.

Step 4: Identify the Function of the Behavior

The underlying purpose for looking at these outcomes is to ultimately determine the function fulfilled by the behavior. These functions generally fall into four categories.

- escape/avoidance—student engages in behavior to escape or avoid an uncomfortable consequence
- attention—student engages in behavior to gain positive or negative attention
- tangible—student engages in behavior to gain a tangible item or reward
- sensory—student engages in behavior to increase sensory input (Crimmins et al., 2007)

After carefully reviewing all the information gathered throughout this process, it is the intervention team's ultimate task to formulate a hypothesis of the purpose that a targeted misbehavior is serving. They can then use this information to change the environmental variables (both antecedent and consequence) to cause a behavior change (Kennedy, 2000). An example of a hypothesis statement is as follows:

[Student's name] engages in [problem behavior] when or after [antecedent], because when he/she does, [typical response]. This is more likely to happen when or because [setting events]. (Crimmins et al., 2007, p. 115).

EXAMPLE: Kayla engages in hitting other students when she perceives that she is receiving insufficient attention, because when she does, other students and the teacher give her attention.

Kayla's teacher will provide frequent feedback during times of appropriate behavior in the classroom. Kayla will receive instruction in peer relations, demonstrating how to gain positive attention from her peers. She will be taught how to approach a student, initiate a conversation, and perhaps gently tap the student on the arm. When Kayla hits other students, she will be removed from the group and not allowed to interact for a period of three minutes.

Teams may occasionally go further and test the hypothesis by manipulating one or more variables (Crimmins et al., 2007; Waguespack et al., 2006). This step is often called functional analysis and may go beyond the typical FBA. Functional analysis is used when students are exhibiting serious and/or destructive behavior and are not responding to intervention methods already tried. It may also be used when the FBA does not provide a clear understanding of the function of the behavior. Parental permission and support should be obtained prior to implementing functional analysis (Janney & Snell, 2008).

In functional analysis the team may establish a series of events in which they alter one factor at a time to determine its affect on the student. This systematic testing of variables is considered very beneficial in determining if the identified function was correct and therefore assists with development of appropriate intensive intervention plans. However, many times in school settings, hypothesis testing is considered unfeasible because it may or may not reduce the problem behavior (Waguespack et al., 2006). As an alternative, teams may alter several variables through an intervention plan in order to increase the likelihood of a behavior change. In the example above, they may alter setting events and antecedents to provide attention during appropriate behavior and alter consequences to remove attention after inappropriate behavior.

One additional step that may be necessary in the case of violent or destructive behavior is to develop a safety plan that can be used whenever necessary. This safety plan should outline procedures for removing the student from situations that threaten his own safety or the safety of others. The plan should identify triggers, both antecedents and setting events, that are likely to cause the student to become violent or destructive. It should also outline ways for the teacher to intervene during times when the behavior is escalating and procedures for ensuring safety during crisis. An excellent example of a safety plan is available from Janney and Snell (2008).

This process of assessment and hypothesis testing through FBA is considered essential in developing effective intervention plans for students in Tier 3 (Ingram et al., 2005; Killu et al., 2006). With some students it is a relatively simple process. However, with others, there may be many contributing factors that make the process very difficult. It can become a very involved process that requires extensive training for at least a portion of the intervention team. IDEA requires that school districts employ professionals who have been properly trained in FBA, and that districts provide ongoing staff development and technical assistance in this type of assessment (Von Ravensberg & Tobin, 2006). Table 5.1 provides a listing of recommended resources for obtaining more specific information on conducting FBAs and tools that may be used in the process.

INTERVENTIONS AND SUPPORTS

Tier 3 interventions are intensive and geared specifically toward the needs of the student. Academic interventions should be designed to provide intensive instruction in the identified deficit area. Behavioral interventions should be based on the function of the behavior identified in the FBA and seek to proactively alter the environmental factors causing the behavior. Both types of interventions should be intensive enough to give adequate instruction, practice, support, and encouragement to the student coupled with frequent progress monitoring (Eber & Hawken, 2008).

Students in Tier 3 should continue to receive universal supports in Tier 1. This layering of support will assist in fading interventions once progress is made (McIntosh et al., 2006). In addition, all classrooms should be structured to promote academic achievement of students with significant behavioral problems (Waguespack et al., 2006). Proactive strategies that provide both behavioral and academic support should be in place in all settings. When appropriate, students in Tier 3 may also access Tier 2 interventions, such as programs for reducing bullying, drug abuse,

Table 5.1   Resources for FBA Information

- Crimmins, D., Farrell, A. F., Smith, P. W., & Bailey, A. (2007). *Positive strategies for students with behavior problems*. Baltimore: Brookes Publishing.
- Marzano, R. J. (2003). *Classroom management that works: Research-based strategies for every teacher*. Alexandria, VA: ASCD
- Janney, R., & Snell, M. E. (2008). *Behavioral support* (2nd ed.). Baltimore: Brookes Publishing.
- Intervention Central
  www.interventioncentral.org/
- Vanderbilt University Center on the Social and
  Emotional Foundations for Early Learning
  www.vanderbilt.edu/csefel/
- Center for Evidence-Based Practice: Young Children With Challenging Behavior
  http://challengingbehavior.fmhi.usf.edu/
- Florida's Positive Behavior Support Project
  http://flpbs.fmhi.usf.edu
- A Research Synthesis on PBS
  http://rrtcpbs.fmhi.usf.edu/rrtcpbsweb/Products/research_synthesis_brief.pdf
- Turning Point Effects for Students With and Without Disabilities Who Are Involved
  in School Disciplinary Actions
  www.education.ucsb.edu/turningpoints/
- Positive Behavioral Interventions and Supports
  www.pbis.org
  - Functional Behavioral Assessment Behavior Support Plan (F-BSP) Protocol
  - Functional Assessment Checklist for Teachers and Staff (FACTS)
- Michigan PBIS Network
  www.bridges4kids.org/PBS/fba.htm
- Virginia Department of Education
  www.ttac.odu.edu/FBA/1FBA%20Intro.htm
- Center for Effective Collaboration and Practice
  http://cecp.air.org/fba/
- Current Issues in Education
  http://cie.asu.edu/volume1/number5/fbacie98.pdf
- Multimodal Functional Behavioral Assessment
  http://mfba.net/forms.html

or violence. Placement in Tier 3 often does not eliminate the need for these types of supports.

As stated previously, behavioral intervention plans for students in Tier 3 should contain one or more very specific interventions based on the function of the behavior identified in the FBA. These interventions may be developed through manipulation of the antecedents and consequences that are impacting the student's behavior. They may include adaptations of interventions or programs that are used in Tier 2. However, the interventions are more individualized and very specific to the presenting behavior problem. Again, this requires expertise on the part of team members. The team should be guided by someone with a strong understanding of behavioral theory and modification techniques.

Modified BEP

One intervention often used in Tier 3 is a modified Behavior Education Program (BEP). The BEP was presented as a Standard Protocol intervention in Tier 2. Students who showed little or no progress when participating in the BEP or whose behavior worsened may benefit from a modified version of the program. This is especially true for students who seek more attention than provided through the Standard Protocol BEP or students who find adult attention aversive or are seeking to avoid adult attention or a task (Crone et al., 2004).

Students who exhibit attention-motivated behavior may not receive enough attention from the standard BEP format. In this case the attention received is not strong enough to change established behaviors. In these instances the BEP may be modified to allow for more frequent interaction during the day. For example, class periods may be divided into smaller segments of time. Students may then receive teacher attention and feedback for behaving appropriately and meeting goals in smaller increments of time. The team may also choose stronger reinforcers for the student. In this case they should evaluate the chosen reinforcers and determine what alternative rewards would provide the necessary amount of reinforcement to the student. These reinforcers may often involve additional or more individual attention from an adult or peer. For example, a student may earn the right to visit with a friend for five minutes in addition to receiving feedback from the teacher and BEP coordinator (Crone et al., 2004).

Students who seek to avoid attention or a task, or who find adult attention aversive may still benefit from a modified BEP. Rather than checking in and out with the BEP coordinator, this student may pick up his Behavior Report Card from a specified location, such as a mailbox within the school. If the student has a close connection with a different adult, it might be appropriate to assign that person for daily check-in and check-out. Students in this category may also benefit from alternative reinforcers, as discussed previously (Crone et al., 2004).

Finally, the BEP may be modified to include academic-related goals for students who have significant academic difficulties. For example, daily goals for the Behavior Report Card could include beginning and ending work on time or bringing materials to class. These goals reinforce academic as well as behavioral functioning. They are very appropriate for students with problems attending, staying focused, or organizing themselves and their materials. The Behavior Report Card will then serve as an ongoing reminder for academic as well as behavioral tasks (Crone et al., 2004).

Other Supports and Interventions

In addition to modified Tier 2 interventions, students in Tier 3 should be provided with individualized interventions designed to respond to their specific needs. These strategies are often viewed in three categories: (1) those designed to *prevent* behaviors from occurring, (2) those designed to *teach* appropriate replacement behaviors, and (3) those designed to *respond* to appropriate behavior by giving students access to the desired function when using the replacement behavior but not when using the inappropriate behavior (Janney & Snell, 2008).

Strategies Designed to Prevent Behaviors by Altering Variables

Tier 3 supports should include interventions designed to alter the antecedents and setting events that trigger the student's behavior problems. The team should have identified these triggers during the FBA process. They should now devise ways of eliminating these triggers or at least substantially reducing their impact. For example, a student who consistently engages in altercations with a particular peer or group of peers may have his schedule changed in order to limit contact with them. A student who has difficulty with transitions may benefit from frequent reminders before an upcoming transition, use of a timer, and a picture or printed schedule showing all transitions. Strategies of this type may also include allowing choice making, providing appropriate educational programming, changing student schedules, or simply "backing off" when it is apparent that the student has experienced an adverse setting event (Janney & Snell, 2008). Regardless of the type of trigger that sparks the behavior, the team can often alter or eliminate the antecedents and setting events in a proactive way in order to avoid the undesired behavior, at least on a temporary basis until replacement behaviors can be mastered (Crimmins et al., 2007). The old adage "choose your battles" is sometimes considered the common-sense approach to altering setting events and antecedents.

Strategies Designed to Teach
Appropriate Replacement Behaviors

In addition to strategies designed to prevent or alter antecedents and setting events, Tier 3 behavior plans should also include direct instruction in replacement behaviors designed to achieve the same function as the target behavior but in a more appropriate way (Janney & Snell, 2008). As discussed in Chapter 4, replacement behaviors give the student a more acceptable alternative to be used in achieving this purpose. These behaviors must be directly taught, modeled, and practiced in order to become part of the student's behavioral repertoire. In our earlier example, Kayla was taught to approach students, initiate conversations, and tap peers on the arm to gain their attention. These replacement behaviors serve the same purpose as hitting students, but result in attention given in a more positive way. By teaching Kayla these behaviors, the teacher is eliminating her need to hit other students.

In addition, students may need to be taught appropriate social skills and expectations. Social skills curricula may be used for this purpose, or students may be given explicit instruction in their natural settings. Students should be taught appropriate behaviors, have those behaviors modeled for them by adults and peers, and be given opportunities to practice them in their daily environment.

Strategies Designed to Respond to Inappropriate Behaviors and Alter Consequences

Responding strategies are designed to alter the consequences experienced by the student after inappropriate behavior. The purpose is to provide more appropriate responses to the replacement behavior than to the inappropriate one. This usually involves the introduction of different consequences. For example, a student may receive a tangible reinforcer after successfully engaging in a desired behavior. When he engages in an undesired behavior, he loses the opportunity to earn that reinforcer (Janney & Snell, 2008).

This process often involves changing the behavior of others who come in contact with the student. For example, peers may need to be taught how to respond and not respond to the student's behaviors. Likewise, teachers often need to be made aware of how their own reaction to misbehavior may actually reinforce that behavior. As stated in earlier examples, students who seek attention often don't care whether the attention they receive is positive or negative. A team may find that the teacher gives individual attention to the student only when he misbehaves. The teacher must make a conscious effort to provide attention when the student is behaving appropriately and limit attention after inappropriate behaviors. When issuing redirection or reprimands, the teacher should limit her attention to the student. This can be difficult, especially when teachers have reached their frustration levels. However, research shows that giving students enthusiastic attention for good behavior and calm, limited attention after inappropriate behavior is much more effective (Sprick et al., 1998). As noted by one behaviorist, there is nothing that excites an adolescent more than turning his or her teacher into a raving maniac!

As you can see, Tier 3 interventions are highly specific, individualized strategies that are based entirely on the student's unique characteristics and needs. These interventions are designed to alter the student's environment as well as their response to environmental factors. They require intensive instruction and support with the ultimate goal of allowing the student to eventually be successful with less support provided through Tiers 1 and 2.

EVALUATION AND FOLLOW-UP

Following the development of the intervention plan, teams should once again take measures to ensure fidelity of implementation. Methods may include observations and checklists. Interventions should be implemented as designed, as often as prescribed, and with consistency.

Data-based decision making is as important in Tier 3 as it was in previous tiers. Data collection should be ongoing and the intervention team should meet frequently to review and evaluate the student's progress. Unsuccessful interventions should be adjusted or changed, constantly responding to assessment data. Curriculum-based measurement is most often used to evaluate the effectiveness of academic interventions. Progress monitoring should occur frequently; weekly or daily assessments yield the most data to assist teams in making decisions. At this level of intensity, teams should pay particular attention to periods of three to five consecutive weeks when students fall consistently below the weekly target or goal. When this occurs, an instructional change should take place. Teachers and interventionists should not continue strategies and interventions that cause no increase in learning (Shores & Chester, 2008; Stecker, 2006).

Tier 3 progress monitoring of behavioral interventions is similar to that used in Tier 2. The team should meet often to review student data. These data should provide a graphic representation of student responsiveness in areas such as number of office discipline referrals or incidence of specific problem behaviors in comparison to the baseline. Behaviors should be evaluated over time. It may be beneficial to determine responsiveness by looking at a time frame rather than daily changes. This will allow the team to determine long-term change. Teachers may document behavior incidences through the same simple means as used in Tier 2.

It is important for teams to understand that many problem behaviors will not be completely extinguished. Research indicates that few problem behaviors are eliminated. It is often appropriate for teams to consider a small but manageable number of these behaviors to be appropriate (Crimmins et al., 2007). For example, a student may never completely quit yelling out in class. However, one or two occurrences in thirty minutes is considered manageable and may actually be similar to the behavior of other students in the classroom.

In addition, teams should review occurrence of replacement behaviors and new skills that are being taught through the intervention plan. The team should establish a goal and then monitor how often the student uses the behavior. Increases in use of replacement behaviors often mirror reductions in inappropriate behaviors.

Finally, teams should monitor the Quality of Life Indicators discussed earlier. Through observations and interviews with the student and family, the team can evaluate changes in relationships, participation, and decision making. The ultimate goal of behavioral supports is to improve the quality of life for the individual (Crimmins et al., 2007). Monitoring the successful improvement of these indicators will bring a sense of purpose and accomplishment to all involved in the planning and intervention process.

As students achieve goals and benchmarks, it is important for the team to determine how to fade supports and foster independence with new skills. Supports should never be removed all at once. Students should receive gradual decreases in support and should be allowed to experience success at each step before having more supports removed. Teams may find that some students will continue to need extensive supports on an ongoing basis.

Planning Through a Wraparound Process

A support tool often used with students with significant behavioral needs in Tier 3 is called a Wraparound (Burns, Schoenwald, Burchard, Faw, & Santos, 2000; Eber & Hawken, 2008; Eber, Sugai, Smith, & Scott, 2002). This is a process used to increase parental involvement in the intervention planning for students with significant behavioral needs and to provide access to supports outside the school setting. It is often initiated when school-level teams identify multiple setting events outside of the school environment that are directly impacting the student's behavior (Eber, Breen, Rose, Unizycki, & London, 2008). The teams are family-centered and include many community representatives and family resources, providing interagency support to students and their families based on the needs of the child and family. The team and plan are culturally relevant and build on strengths present within the family, the student, and the service providers (Eber & Hawken, 2008).

Wraparound has been found to be highly successful for students with significant needs, such as those with extreme emotional and/or behavioral problems. It has been shown to decrease restrictive placements, including residential placements, for many students. Additionally, it is associated with improved behavioral, academic, and post-school adjustment factors for students with significant needs (Burns et al., 2000; Eber et al., 2002). It is considered to be appropriate for 1–2 percent of students with the most significant needs (Eber et al., 2008).

The Wraparound process is described as follows: it "brings teachers, families, and community representatives together to commit unconditionally to a way of conducting problem solving and planning that gives equal importance and support to the child and his or her family, teachers, and other caregivers. A key element is blending perspectives to achieve consensus on specific and individualized desired outcomes" (Eber et al., 2002, p. 173). The process is run by a trained facilitator. The facilitator uses specific techniques to engage the student, families, and others in building a strong support network (Eber et al., 2008). Supports for the student and family may include respite, mentoring, housing, transportation, employment assistance, childcare, or healthcare. Supports for the school may include consultation and technical assistance for teachers, functional behavioral assessment, and instructional plans for academic, behavioral, and social skills (Eber et al., 2002). Due to its focus on variables outside the educational system, this approach is somewhat unique to schools. However, it is similar to transition planning for students with disabilities.

As stated earlier, Wraparound processes should be led by a trained and highly skilled facilitator. It should not be attempted without intensive training and preparation. When used, school-based team members must be diligent about identifying community and family supports and providers who should be included in the process (Eber et al., 2002). There are numerous resources available for schools interested in learning more about the process. Some of these are included in Table 5.2.

Table 5.2   Resources for Wraparound Process

- National Wraparound Initiative
  www.rtc.pdx.edu/nwi/
- University of Kansas, Center on Developmental Disabilities—
  Positive Behavior Support
  http://uappbs.apbs.org/
- Kansas Institute for Positive Behavior Support
  www.kipbsmodules.org
- Illinois PBIS Network
  www.pbisillinois.org/

CASE STUDY OF A STUDENT RECEIVING TIER 3 INTERVENTIONS

J. C. is a 12-year-old boy who has received Tier 2 interventions since the beginning of the school year. He lives with his grandmother and two older brothers in an urban area of the Midwest. He exhibits multiple behavioral problems at school, including defiance, aggression toward other students, and noncompliance with school rules. He was retained in second grade. He is currently in fifth grade.

J. C. has received seven office discipline referrals this school year (September through March). His teacher identified numerous factors that place J. C. at risk for behavioral problems. These include absence of parental control, poverty, and history of child abuse from birth parents. In addition, his academic functioning is below grade level. J. C.'s oral reading fluency is measured at 45 words per minute (wpm). Students at fifth-grade level should read approximately 130 wpm (Hosp, Hosp, & Howell, 2007). His reading comprehension is measured at third-grade level. J. C. is also below grade level in math, with deficits in problem solving and numbers/operations.

The Student Assistance Team has met approximately once each month since October. During the past three weeks, they have conducted a functional behavioral assessment. Assessment tools included teacher completion of the Systematic Screening for Behavior Disorders, interval recording of noncompliance, documentation of Antecedent-Behavior-Consequence, and observations by the school psychologist and behavioral specialist.

J. C. received academic interventions in both reading and math as part of his Tier 2 intervention plan. At that time J. C. gained 28 wpm in twenty-four weeks of targeted instruction. He made no significant gains in reading comprehension, numbers and operations, or problem solving.

J. C. has also participated in his school's Behavior Education Program since January. The intervention resulted in no reduction in problem behaviors. In fact, during February and March, there was a 15 percent increase in documented incidences of aggression and noncompliance. During the past two weeks, J. C. has exhibited a baseline of eight verbal outbursts during one-hour instructional periods. These outbursts usually occurred when he was given an assignment. They most often resulted in removal from the classroom.

The Student Assistance Team, including J. C.'s grandmother, met to discuss assessment results and form a hypothesis regarding the function of the problem behavior. It was determined that J. C.'s noncompliance may be, in part, a result of task avoidance. The team determined that J. C. should receive individualized tutoring as a Tier 3 intervention. Instruction will be provided by the reading coach during the school day for sixty minutes each day. The team chose to focus on reading instruction first and will consider math instruction after four weeks of adjustment to the intervention process. Further educational evaluation will be conducted during the next few weeks.

J. C. will participate in a modified Behavior Education Program in which he may receive reinforcement eight times throughout each day for mastery of a goal during a fourty-five minute time frame. In addition, teachers will become more cognizant of setting events and antecedents that often trigger behavioral problems. J. C. often becomes defiant when given the same assignments as other students. Teachers will provide J. C. with assignments that are shorter and provide opportunities for success. Instruction will be differentiated to allow for different response modes and altered tasks. In addition, teachers will give J. C. individual assistance with reading and understanding directions.

The school counselor will work with J. C. to help him learn appropriate ways of expressing frustration and anger. J. C. will participate in a social skills group that meets twice each week. Teachers will encourage J. C. to use these alternative behaviors in the classroom. A reward system was established for use throughout the day. J. C. chose time in the school gym as his reinforcer. He may earn one minute of gym time for every fifteen minutes in which he has no outbursts. In addition, J. C. may earn one additional minute each time he uses an appropriate alternative behavior. He may use the time when ten minutes have accumulated.

Community resources were identified and set up to support J. C. and his family. J. C.'s grandmother, Ms. Ramirez, identified several areas in which she felt she needed assistance. These included location of safe affordable housing, childcare during school holidays so that she can work, and counseling services to assist J. C. and his brothers in coming to terms with their parents' imprisonment. A representative from social services will assist J. C.'s grandmother in locating these resources. In addition, the school will provide afterschool care through an existing program for J. C. and his brothers. J. C. will receive an additional thirty minutes of tutoring each day through the afterschool program. Other resources, such as participation in a Big Brother program, will be explored. The team will meet again in two weeks to discuss J. C.'s progress.

SUMMARY

Planning for students with significant behavioral problems is a difficult task. However, it can be greatly enhanced and outcomes can be positive when teams take steps to consider all variables including home and community factors, student and parent values, and available support systems. Teams should follow a problem-solving process that begins with Functional

Behavioral Assessment. This assessment should lead to an observable and measurable definition of the behavior, including baseline data. It should identify antecedents and setting events that trigger the inappropriate behavior. In addition, it should identify consequences that reinforce the behavior and cause it to continue. Information about these variables should assist the team in determining the function of the behavior.

After gathering this data, the team should identify interventions that are appropriate for reducing the problem behavior and increasing the occurrence of more accepted replacement behaviors. These interventions may be a modification of a previously established research-based intervention or they may involve manipulation of the variables outlined above. This planning process should be led by one or more persons trained in behavior modification.

Finally, student response to interventions should be carefully monitored. Decisions regarding the continued need for supports and interventions should be based on individual student data and achievement indicators. The intervention plan should be continually adjusted to reflect the student's changing needs.

CONCLUSION

This book has focused on using the RTI process to address both academic and behavioral problems in one unified comprehensive model. Emphasis has been placed on development of a behavioral framework to complement academic programs that may already be established within a school. The academic and behavioral frameworks have many similarities. In fact, the essential elements are the same for both: increasingly intensive research-based interventions, universal screening and ongoing progress monitoring, and measures to ensure fidelity of instruction. These similarities make it possible to combine the separate features into one unified model, providing a seamless process for improving student achievement and behavior. Research shows that this is the most effective way to implement RTI.

Schools and districts should invest considerable time and resources into the building of a strong foundation for RTI implementation. Leadership teams should be involved in long-range planning, promoting buy-in from all stakeholders, and identifying resources necessary for appropriate implementation. They should also assess school culture and prepare the school for the change process. RTI is most successful when embraced by the entire faculty, parents, students, and community as a worthwhile school improvement process.

Research-based interventions vary somewhat between the two sides of the unified model. Many behavioral interventions have been researched using single-subject design or case studies. OSEP's Center on Positive Behavioral Interventions and Supports recommends that teams closely monitor these strategies for their effectiveness and appropriateness for individual students. Most students progress through each tier when receiving academic interventions. This may not be the case for students with behavioral difficulties.

Tier 1 interventions involve effective instruction in the general education classroom. This instruction should be differentiated to meet a variety of student needs. Teachers should use data from formative assessment to make instructional decisions. Preassessment should be used to plan instruction and place students in flexible groups. Behaviorial expectations should be directly taught for instructional and transition periods. School-wide expectations should promote consistency throughout common areas of the school.

Tier 2 interventions should target specific deficit skills in students at risk for academic or behavioral difficulties. Tier 1 universal screening measures identify these students and Tier 2 interventions should be provided immediately. Interventions at this level are most often provided in small groups. Frequent progress monitoring should drive instruction through the use of effective data-based decision making.

Tier 3 should involve intensive, individualized supports and interventions, again targeted to specific deficit areas. The interventions should be of sufficient intensity and duration to bring about legitimate, enduring results. With some students, this may require locating resources and supports outside of the school, especially when working with students with extreme behaviors.

Throughout the pyramid, steps should be taken to measure and ensure fidelity of instruction and intervention implementation. This may involve the use of skill-specific checklists, faculty observations, or self-assessment checklists. This step is imperative in ensuring that all students have received appropriate instruction and supports, ruling out the lack of instruction as the cause for the deficit.

When incorporated into all aspects of the school, including curriculum, assessment, resources, personnel, and staff development, the RTI process has proven to be a highly successful vehicle for school improvement. As school leadership and faculties seek to meet legal requirements and provide an appropriate education for all students, they should structure their efforts around a comprehensive plan for RTI implementation.

Resource A

Process Development Tools

COMPREHENSIVE RESPONSE TO INTERVENTION NEEDS ASSESSMENT

	Current level of implementation? 1 = None 2 = Beginning 3 = Advanced 4 = Completed	Priority (Rank order for each section)	Specific components that are in place	Specific components that are needed
Readiness for Change—This section applies to both district- and building-level leadership.				
Leadership team has been formed and includes representatives from all key stakeholder groups.				
Data analysis has been performed and indicated the need for change.				
Gap analysis has been performed to identify areas of change needed.				
Leadership team has developed vision for expected outcomes.				
Leadership team has developed short-term and long-term action plans for district implementation.				
Faculty and staff have embraced vision and are ready to begin RTI implementation as a school improvement process.				
Initial information has been shared with parents and the community.				

	Current level of implementation? 1 = None 2 = Beginning 3 = Advanced 4 = Completed	Priority (Rank order for each section)	Specific components that are in place	Specific components that are needed
The entire administration portrays to the staff, students, and parents the importance of the RTI process for increased student achievement.				
Tier 1 Universal Supports				
All teachers are effectively trained in the curriculum standards for the grade level and content area in which they teach.				
Curriculum standards are implemented as designed in each content area.				
Teachers have a thorough understanding and knowledge of the principles and strategies of differentiated instruction.				
Instruction is differentiated by content, process, and product on a consistent and ongoing basis.				
Curriculum mapping is utilized to align the curriculum across grade levels and content areas.				
Eighty percent of students meet or exceed standards in each content area.				

(Continued)

(Continued)

	Current level of implementation? 1 = None 2 = Beginning 3 = Advanced 4 = Completed	Priority (Rank order for each section)	Specific components that are in place	Specific components that are needed
Tier 1 Universal Supports (Continued)				
Staff development plan has been developed for both short-term and long-term implementation.				
A school-wide behavioral plan is in place that contains clearly established expectations, rewards, and consequences.				
Eighty to ninety percent of students are successful with the school-wide behavioral plan.				
Each classroom has in place a management plan that mirrors the school-wide behavioral plan.				
School-wide, class-wide, and individual student behavioral data are consistently monitored and analyzed.				
Universal Screening/Progress Monitoring				
Universal screening is used to identify all students at risk for academic and behavioral problems.				
Curriculum-based measurement (CBM) is used frequently to assess student academic progress.				

	Current level of implementation? 1 = None 2 = Beginning 3 = Advanced 4 = Completed	Priority (Rank order for each section)	Specific components that are in place	Specific components that are needed
Universal Screening/Progress Monitoring (Continued)				
Teachers are trained in the use of curriculum-based measurement to evaluate student learning.				
Teachers have curriculum-based measurement tools available to them in their content area and appropriate grade level.				
Teachers understand how to analyze, chart, and interpret data.				
Teachers utilize data from ongoing curriculum-based measurement to drive instructional decisions on a daily and/or weekly basis.				
Teachers have behavioral checklists available to identify students with internalizing behaviors.				
Tier 2 Targeted Interventions				
The school has in place standard protocol interventions designed to address common and/or frequent learning or behavior problems.				
Teachers and interventionists have knowledge base of multiple research-based interventions to address a wide variety of learning and behavior problems.				

(Continued)

(Continued)

Tier 2 Targeted Interventions (Continued)	Current level of implementation? 1 = None 2 = Beginning 3 = Advanced 4 = Completed	Priority (Rank order for each section)	Specific components that are in place	Specific components that are needed
Teachers and interventionists have resources available to train them in specific research-based interventions as needed.				
Teachers and interventionists implement research-based interventions in their classroom with integrity and fidelity.				
Flexible scheduling for students and staff is utilized to enable student access to standard protocols.				
Job responsibilities have been restructured to enable student access to standard protocols.				
A process is in place to ensure research-based interventions are implemented with fidelity.				
Student response to intervention is assessed through frequent progress monitoring.				
Data-based decision making is consistently used to make programming decisions for students.				

	Current level of implementation? 1 = None 2 = Beginning 3 = Advanced 4 = Completed	Priority (Rank order for each section)	Specific components that are in place	Specific components that are needed
Tier 3 Intensive Supports (Continued)				
Problem-solving teams are used for student planning.				
Intensive individualized instruction is available to students as needed.				
Individualized assessment is available when needed (FBA, psychological evaluations, etc.).				
Frequent progress monitoring and data review are used for student planning.				
Research-based interventions are used for intensive supports.				
Community supports are identified and included in planning process as needed.				
Ongoing Process Development				
The school schedule is designed to provide for flexibility and restructuring of resources to meet student needs.				

(Continued)

(Continued)

Ongoing Process Development (Continued)	Current level of implementation? 1 = None 2 = Beginning 3 = Advanced 4 = Completed	Priority (Rank order for each section)	Specific components that are in place	Specific components that are needed
Various strategies including walk-throughs, extended observations, teacher conferences, lesson plan evaluations, and others are used to monitor implementation of instruction and supports.				
A variety of resources are identified and provided to address deficit areas in curriculum, behavior management, and instructional strategies.				
Teachers are provided with time and incentives for collaboration, professional growth, and staff development.				
School and class data are analyzed to determine areas of need.				
Adequate and appropriate resources to address identified needs are provided to staff.				
Action plans are updated at least annually to guide implementation in future years.				

GAP ANALYSIS FORM

Leadership teams may use this form to examine existing programs and determine gaps in instructional and behavioral supports. Results may be used in establishing the need for a comprehensive RTI model and in developing an action plan.

Area of Need	Program or Process That Addresses That Need	Targeted Population	Effectiveness of Program	Deficits Still Present That Could Be Addressed Through RTI	Goal

DISTRICT IMPLEMENTATION CHECKLIST FOR EFFECTIVE RTI

1. Form a district-level leadership team composed of key stakeholders.
   a. Superintendent
   b. District-level administrators in curriculum, instruction, assessment, special education, student support services, ELL, Title I, human resources, fiscal services, etc.
   c. Building principals
   d. Building-level curriculum experts including instructional coaches
   e. Student support services personnel, such as school psychologists
   f. Key teacher leaders
   g. Community representatives
   h. Parent representatives
2. Develop readiness for change with district leadership team.
   a. Identify the need for change. Evaluate student performance to determine how many students could receive benefit from the process.
   b. Complete a gap analysis to identify current program strengths and weaknesses.
   c. Develop vision for the expected outcomes.
   d. Analyze data to determine strengths, weaknesses, and potential impact.
   e. Identify state requirements and timelines.
3. Develop district action plan for RTI implementation.
   a. Provide thorough training in the RTI process and its essential components to members of the leadership team.
   b. Complete needs assessment to determine current levels of implementation.
   c. Identify RTI framework to be used (academic, behavioral, comprehensive).
   d. Identify and address concerns.
   e. Identify which schools will be involved in initial and secondary phases of implementation.
   f. Identify necessary commitments in terms of staff development, materials, assessment tools, and additional resources.
   g. Identify barriers to implementation and develop plans for resolution.
   h. Develop timeline for implementation.

4. Develop building leadership team composed of key stakeholders.
   a. Core membership from school that served on district team.
   b. Additional members to represent all groups involved.
5. Develop building action plan for implementation.
   a. Follow procedures similar to district team.
   b. Adjust and refine plan for individual school needs.
6. Begin initial training for participating faculty and staff.
   a. Provide in-service training in small segments, providing time to synthesize and apply information to curricular requirements.
   b. Provide opportunities for practice, modeling, and coaching of new skills.
7. Communicate information to parents regarding the overall structure of the RTI model.
   a. Include information in student handbook.
   b. Share information at parent meetings, such as PTA.
   c. Highlight interventions that could be utilized by parents in regular communication tools, such as newsletters.
8. Evaluate and strengthen Tier 1 instruction and supports, ensuring fidelity of curriculum implementation.
   a. Ensure that instruction is differentiated and appropriate for at least 80 percent of general education students.
   b. Ensure that school-wide behavioral plan is effective for 80–90 percent of students.
   c. Identify staff development needs to strengthen Tier 1.
   d. Provide identified staff development.
   e. Choose universal screening and progress monitoring tools.
   f. Implement universal screening to identify students at risk.
9. Develop structure for Tier 2 targeted interventions.
   a. Identify research-based interventions appropriate for student needs.
   b. Develop schedule that provides time and resources for Tier 2 interventions.
   c. Provide intervention training to individuals who will carry out Tier 2 instruction and supports.
   d. Identify and acquire progress monitoring tools and procedures.
   e. Provide professional development on progress monitoring.
10. Implement Tier 2 interventions with at-risk students.
    a. Implement intervention plans as designed.
    b. Evaluate progress frequently and consistently.
    c. Ensure fidelity of interventions.
    d. Communicate plan and results with parents on a regular basis.

11. Develop structure for Tier 3 practices.
    a. Identify research-based interventions appropriate for student needs.
    b. Develop schedule that provides time and resources for Tier 3 interventions.
    c. Use student data to develop data-driven IEPs when appropriate.
    d. Implement Tier 3 interventions.
    e. Evaluate progress frequently and consistently.
    f. Adjust instruction and supports based on data.
    g. Ensure fidelity of interventions.
    h. Communicate plan and results with parents on a regular basis.
12. Provide support for continual evaluation and improvement of process.
    a. Provide ongoing staff development.
    b. Engage in continuous evaluation of quality of instruction and supports in Tiers 1, 2 and 3.
    c. Evaluate effectiveness of interventions.
    d. Evaluate student data to refine action plan.
    e. Allocate additional resources as needed.
    f. Adjust district policies as needed.

SOURCE: Adapted from Gorton, R., Alston, J. A., & Snowden, P. (2007). *School leadership and administration: Important concepts, case studies, and simulations* (7th ed.). New York: McGraw-Hill. National Staff Development Council. (2001).

SAMPLE MULTIYEAR PLAN FOR DISTRICT IMPLEMENTATION

This multiyear plan is appropriate for implementing an academic framework, a behavioral framework, or both concurrently.

RTI Component	Year 1	Year 2	Year 3	Year 4
Form district leadership team	X			
Develop readiness for change with district team	X			
Develop and refine district action plan	X	X	X	X
Develop building leadership teams	P	X		
Develop building action plan	P	X		
Begin initial training for faculty and staff	P	X		
Communicate information to parents	X	X	X	X
Evaluate and strengthen Tier 1 supports	X	X	X	X
Identify and acquire/develop universal screening tools	X			
Implement universal screening	P	X		
Identify and acquire/develop progress monitoring tools	P	X		
Develop structure for Tier 2 targeted interventions and supports		P	X	
Identify research-based interventions	X	X	X	X
Train service providers in research-based interventions	P	X	X	X
Implement Tier 2 interventions and supports		P	X	
Implement progress monitoring		P	X	
Develop structure for Tier 3 interventions and supports		P	X	
Implement Tier 3 Structure			P	X

X—full implementation

P—implementation in pilot schools only

SAMPLE MULTIYEAR PLAN FOR STAFF DEVELOPMENT

Staff Development Topic	Year 1	Year 2	Year 3	Year 4
RTI process overview	A			
RTI intensive training	DL, BL, P	A		
Differentiated instruction and Tier 1 instructional components (will vary based on needs of district)	A	A	A	A
Problem solving and collaboration	A	A	A	A
Benchmark assessment	DL, BL, P	A		
Curriculum-based measurement and other progress monitoring tools	DL, BL, P	A	A	A
Research-based interventions	DL, BL, P	A	A	A
Data-driven instructional practices	DL, BL, P	A	A	A
School-wide behavioral plan		DL, BL, P	A	A
Targeted behavioral interventions		DL, BL, P	A	A

DL—District Leadership

BL—Building Leadership

P—Pilot Schools

A—All Schools

Resource B

Tools for Tier 1

QUALITY OF TIER 1 INSTRUCTION RUBRIC

Teacher: _____ School: _____

Observer: _____

Category	3	2	1	0
Core Instruction	Curriculum standards are taught with fidelity to high levels of understanding using a variety of effective and appropriate resources.	Curriculum standards are taught with fidelity to high levels of understanding using resources required by district.	Curriculum standards are taught to all students.	Curriculum standards are not being taught effectively.
Differentiation in the Lesson	Differentiation is evident in the areas of content, process, product, and learning environment.	Differentiation is evident in two or three areas.	Differentiation is evident in one area.	There is no differentiation evident in any of the areas.
Grouping Variations	A variety of grouping strategies are demonstrated based on interests, multiple intelligences, learning styles, ability, and/or other criteria.	There are two to three group activities based on ability or random groupings.	There is one group activity based on _____ groupings.	No groups are utilized in this lesson.
Backward Design	Assessment is developed before instructional activities and outlines what the teacher wants students to know, do, and understand.	Assessment reflects what the teacher wants students to know, do, and understand.	The lesson plan reflects what the teacher wants the students to know, do, and understand for every unit.	There is no evidence of Backward Design.
Student Assessment	Students are preassessed for readiness, interest, and learning profiles.	Students are preassessed in two areas.	Students are preassessed in one area.	There is no evidence of preassessment.

Category	3	2	1	0
Student Assessment	A variety of formal and informal assessments are utilized before, during, and after the teaching of the unit. Informal assessments are used daily to assist in planning for the next day's lessons.	A variety of formal and informal assessments are utilized before, during, and after the teaching of the unit. Informal assessments are used every two to four days to assist in planning.	Informal assessments are incorporated into some parts of the lesson. Formal assessments show some differentiation.	There is no evidence of informal assessments. Formal assessments are the same for all students.
Student Assessment	Assessment uses a variety of formats including performance tasks.	Assessment includes at least one performance task per unit.	Assessment includes one performance task per semester.	No performance tasks are used.
Tiered Instruction	Lessons are tiered to address all levels of functioning.	All student-centered activities or assignments show evidence of tiered instruction.	At least one activity or assignment shows evidence of tiered instruction.	There is no evidence of tiered instruction.
Scaffolding Support	Scaffolding and support is provided for various students throughout the lesson.	Scaffolding and support is provided for various students during assignments.	Scaffolding and support is provided only for students with disabilities.	There is no evidence of scaffolding or support in the lesson.
Classroom Management	Expectations are taught directly and explicitly for instructional and transition times. Cues such as posters or bulletin boards reinforce expectations.	Expectations are taught directly and explicitly for instructional and transition times. Expectations are reinforced periodically.	Students have understanding of and follow expectations.	There is no evidence that students understand expectations.

BEHAVIOR MATRIX

This behavior matrix was developed for middle school implementation. The four components form an acronym for the school's mascot (CATS).

	Cooperate	Act With Appropriate Attitude	Take Responsibility	Show Respect
Classroom	• Follow directions the first time • Stay on task • Speak appropriately • Follow rules • Stay in assigned area	• Show eagerness to learn • Speak positively toward both teachers and students	• Bring all needed materials • Be prepared • Complete all assignments on time • Keep classroom area clean	• Leave property of others alone • Respect personal space
Assemblies Extracurricular	• Be attentive to the program • Follow directions • Participate when asked	• Exhibit school pride and spirit • Demonstrate good sportsmanship • Use only positive responses	• Be on time, keep area clean • Keep hands and feet to yourself • Move orderly and quietly • Stay in assigned areas	• Listen/focus on speaker • Follow directions • Respect others' space
Field Trips	• Be on time • Be ready to participate and enjoy the field trip	• Show school pride in community • Show self-respect by being clean and dressing neatly	• Notify parents of pick-up time • Turn in paperwork on time • Follow all bus rules	• Follow directions the first time • Keep hands, feet, and objects to self • Be attentive when someone is speaking
Gym/Locker Room	• Dress out daily • Participate daily	• Keep hands to yourself • Keep belongings secure • Turn in lost items	• Use and take care of equipment as intended • Be in roll call on time • Keep locker room clean	• Follow directions the first time • Leave property of others alone • Encourage peer participation
Cafeteria/Patio	• Stay in line • Chew food with mouth closed • Food goes from plate to fork to mouth	• Use quiet voices • Clean your area • Choose healthy foods	• Keep area clean • Keep food and drinks in the cafeteria • Know your number	• Quickly and quietly through the line • Leave area neat and clean • Take and eat only your food • Stay in your assigned area

	Cooperate	Act With Appropriate Attitude	Take Responsibility	Show Respect
Restroom	• Dispose of paper towels in trash container • Choose it, use it, flush it • Wash hands	• Mind your own business • Return to learn • Report acts of vandalism	• Have a signed agenda/pass • Keep restroom clean and floor dry • Return to class ASAP	• Leave others alone • Be quick and quiet
Media Center	• Use quiet voice • Have permission to go	• Have a purpose • Wait patiently for assistance	• Bring signed agenda/pass • Return books on time • Bring needed items • Ask for help if needed	• Sign in and out • Take care of all materials • Use appropriate language • Follow directions the first time
Hallway	• Keep hands, feet, and objects to yourself • Leave room for others to pass	• Keep hallway clean • Keep lockers and walls clean	• Have a signed agenda/pass during class time • Stay in designated area	• Keep hands, feet, and objects away from others, walls, and displays • Use quiet voices • Walk on right side of hallway
Office	• State purpose politely • Exit when business is completed	• State purpose politely • Wait patiently	• Have signed permission to come to office • Walk directly to the office	• Wait your turn • Ask permission to use the phone • Be polite to office staff
Arrival/Dismissal for Car and Bus	• Walk directly to designated area • Follow directions the first time • Keep hands, feet, and objects to yourself	• Be courteous to other riders • Follow directions the first time	• Stay in designated area • Stay seated at all times • Follow bus rules • When late to school, an adult must sign you in at the office	• Use quiet voices • Keep hands, feet, and objects to yourself • Have permission to leave the assigned area
Locker Breaks	• Go straight to locker • Get to class on time • Follow directions the first time	• Wait your turn • Be helpful when needed • Concentrate on designated task	• Get necessary items for each class • Keep locker neat and organized • Move quickly from locker to class	• Be polite • Keep area clean

REWARD MENU FOR "CATS CASH"

Patio Pass—15 CC per student

Used only on a day when it is not raining or wet outside. This day will be designated each month and will be announced. Student must give Cats Cash to teacher he or she has for lunch prior to going to the patio to eat. A staff member would need to be outside to supervise. Students are to remain seated at the tables while outside. All trash must be collected and disposed of when coming inside.

Eat Lunch With a Friend in Lunchroom—10 CC

Student must give Cats Cash to teacher and get teacher's approval before sitting with a friend at a table other than the one assigned. Students must follow all lunchroom expectations while at the friend's table. Student must leave with his or her regular class.

Teacher's Aide—15 CC

This must be arranged at least a day before it is to occur. The teacher of the class the student is missing and the teacher who the student wants to aid must approve beforehand in writing. Student must give Cats Cash to teacher of the class he or she is missing. Student is required to make up any missed work from the class.

Hat Day Pass—10 CC

This item is only available on designated hat days, not every school day. Student must give Cats Cash to the teacher who is collecting money for the hat day sticker.

Athletic Event Pass—15 CC

This item is only available at home events. Student must give Cats Cash to the teacher who is collecting money at the gate of the event.

Activity in Gym During Homeroom—10 CC

This will occur on a designated day each month and will be announced letting everyone know when it will occur. Student must give Cats Cash to homeroom teacher and get teacher's approval and pass before going to the gym. The pass must be presented when entering the back door of the gym.

Demerit Pass—20 CC

Students may eliminate a demerit by giving the Cats Cash to the teacher when the demerit is being issued. The demerit form will still be completed by the teacher noting the behavior infraction and will be filed with the redeemed Cats Cash attached by the student's team leader for data purposes.

Outside Reward Time—15 CC

This will occur on a designated day each month and will be announced letting everyone know when it will occur. This will occur during team time and each team will determine when they will go outside. Student must give Cats Cash to homeroom teacher to participate.

Dance Pass—15 CC

This item may be used to gain admittance into any of the scheduled school-wide dances. Student should give the Cats Cash to the person collecting the money at the entrance to the gym.

Late Homework Pass—5 CC

This item can be redeemed on a day that a homework assignment is due. The student must complete a Late Homework Pass form, staple the Cats Cash to the form, and turn in the form to the teacher that day in class. The student then has three school days to turn in the completed homework assignment with no late points being deducted.

Pay Media Center Fine—1 CC

A student may redeem Cats Cash to pay a media center fine. For this reward 1 Cats Cash is equivalent to $.25 worth of library fines. Student must present the Cats Cash to the media center staff.

Pencil Purchase—2 CC

Some teachers may allow a student to redeem Cats Cash for a pencil if they are unprepared. The student can present the Cats Cash to the teacher for a pencil. If the student does not have Cats Cash, the teacher may loan them a pencil but will make a checkmark in their records.

Locker Pass—2 CC

Some teachers may allow a student to redeem Cats Cash in order to go to their locker to get school-related items that they need for class purposes. Student must ask the teacher if they can go back to their locker to get said item(s) and must then pay the Cats Cash to the teacher.

School Store Items—Varying CC

Students may purchase school store items when the store is open. The amount of Cats Cash needed to purchase will vary depending on the item. Student should give the Cats Cash to the staff member running the store.

Gift Card Drawing—1 CC

Instead of redeeming their Cats Cash for the above reward items, students may have their Cats Cash entered into a weekly drawing for a $25 gift card of their choice. This drawing will occur every Friday during morning announcements. Students can enter as many Cats Cash as they wish, thus increasing their odds of winning. During the last week of each grading period there will be three $100 gift card winners drawn. In this drawing there will be one winner from each grade level.

ALL ITEMS ARE SUBJECT TO TEACHER DISCRETION

BEHAVIOR LEVELS

Level I

Level I behaviors are minor rule violations that will result in an immediate verbal correction by an adult school employee (administrator, teacher, paraprofessional, custodian, bus driver, secretary, or cafeteria worker) and possible consequences.

These offenses will not result in an immediate office referral.

Infractions

- No materials
- Tardy
- Minor dress code violations
- Minor hall infractions
- Talking/off task
- Dishonesty/cheating
- Failure to follow directions or rules
- Running, pushing, or shoving
- Horseplay
- Disrespectful/unkind to students
- Without a pass signed by a teacher
- Inappropriate language to students

Consequences

When problems do arise in your class:
First, make sure the student understands what the problem is and allow him or her a chance to get out of the situation. How? Reward/praise those behaving appropriately (give them the attention) to see if they correct their behavior. Second, *Reteach* the appropriate behavior using the Behavior Matrix, *Reinforce*, *Reward*.

Remaining Options

- Warnings
- Student–teacher conference
- Demerit (must have parent contact documented on each demerit sheet)
- Team conference with student
- Parent conference
- Referral for SST
- Probation period

- Minor work detail
- Afterschool detention
- Change seating chart to move student
- Notes to parent signed and returned; phone calls whenever possible. Consult your team members for help with problem students.

Level II

Level II behaviors are more serious in nature. Level II behaviors will result in an immediate verbal correction by an adult school employee (administrator, teacher, paraprofessional, custodian, bus driver, secretary, or cafeteria worker) and a logical consequence.

Infractions

- Chronic Level I behavior
- Defiance of authority
- Disrespect for authority
- Chronic dress code infractions
- Inappropriate computer use
- Inappropriate display of affection
- Profanity
- Racial or ethnic slurs
- Skipping class
- Stealing
- Being in an unauthorized area
- Physical aggression toward students
- Bus infraction

Consequences

- Office referral
- Bus intervention
- Bus suspension
- ISS
- OSS
- Administrative contact with parent
- Administrative conference with parent
- Restitution
- Referral for SST
- Behavior correction plan
- Parent escort at school

Level III

Level III behaviors are extremely serious and illegal behaviors. Most of these behaviors violate the dignity, well-being, and safety of others. These behaviors will not be tolerated at school. Level III will result in immediate enforcement of logical consequences including contacting law enforcement officials.

Infractions

- Chronic/extreme Level II behavior
- Fighting/striking back
- Bullying/harassment of other students
- Verbal/written implied threats of violence
- Physical aggression toward authority
- Assault of teachers or other authority
- Vandalism
- Theft from authority or school
- Possession of inappropriate items
- Possession of tobacco or related items
- Possession of over-the-counter drugs
- Possession of prescription drugs
- Possession of imitation drugs
- Possession of illegal drugs
- Possession of drug-related items
- Possession of alcohol
- Unauthorized exit from class or school property
- Destruction of property
- Computer trespass
- Sexual misconduct/harassment

Consequences

- Immediate office referral
- Any Level II consequence
- Long-term OSS/ISS
- Referral to tribunal
- Contact law enforcement
- Contact district attorney
- Probable legal charges filed
- Probable arrest
- Probable court appearance
- Probable probation assignment
- Possible jail time

DISCIPLINE REFERRAL FORM

Student name: _____ Grade: 6   7   8

Date: _____ Time: _____

Referring staff: _____ Team: _____

Location

❏ Bathroom	❏ Bus	❏ Cafeteria
❏ Classroom	❏ Gym	❏ Hallway
❏ Library	❏ Arrival/Dismissal	
❏ Special Event	❏ Other: _____	

Level II Behavior	Level III Behavior	Possible Motivation
❏ Chronic Level I behavior	❏ Chronic/extreme Level II behavior	❏ Obtain peer attention
❏ Defiance/disrespect of authority	❏ Fighting/striking back	❏ Obtain adult attention
❏ Chronic dress code infractions	❏ Bullying/harassment of other students	❏ Obtain item/activities
❏ Inappropriate computer use	❏ Verbal/written implied threats of violence	❏ Avoid peer(s)
❏ Inappropriate display of affection		❏ Avoid adult
❏ Profanity/racial or ethnic slurs	❏ Physical aggression toward authority	❏ Avoid task or activity
❏ Skipping class	❏ Assault of teachers/other authority	❏ Don't know
❏ Stealing	❏ Vandalism	❏ Other_____
❏ Being in an unauthorized area	❏ Theft from authority/school	_____
❏ Physical aggression toward students	❏ Possession of	_____
	❏ Inappropriate items	
Others Involved	❏ Tobacco	**Office Use Only Consequence**
	❏ Alcohol	
❏ None	❏ Drugs of any kind: _____	❏ Loss of privilege
❏ Peer(s)	_____(specify)	❏ Parent contact
❏ Staff	❏ Unauthorized exit from class/school property	❏ Conference/warning
❏ Teacher		❏ In-school suspension
❏ Substitute	❏ Destruction of property	❏ Out-of-school suspension
❏ Other	❏ Computer trespass	❏ Reimbursement
❏ Unknown	❏ Sexual misconduct/harassment	❏ Other _____

Names of all witnesses: _____

_____

Other comments: _____

_____

_____

Administrator's signature: _____

Comments: _____

_____

_____

SIMPLE DATA COLLECTION FORM

Student name: _____ Date: _____

Observer: _____

Data collection method: _____

_____

Time Frame					
Activity					
Behavior					

Anecdotal information: _____

_____

_____

_____

_____

_____

_____

_____

_____

_____

_____

_____

_____

_____

_____

_____

_____

_____

DEMERIT PLAN

Student name: _____ Date issued: _____

1 demerit	Parent/guardian contact and warning to student
2 demerits	Parent/guardian contact and silent lunch
3 demerits	Parent/guardian contact, team meeting with student during connections, and silent lunch
4 demerits	Parent/guardian contact and in-team suspension
5 demerits	Office referral (in-school suspension)

Infractions
- ❏ No materials
- ❏ Tardy
- ❏ Minor dress code violations
- ❏ Minor hall infractions
- ❏ Talking/off task
- ❏ Dishonesty/cheating
- ❏ Failure to follow directions or rules
- ❏ Running, pushing, or shoving
- ❏ Horseplay
- ❏ Disrespectful/unkind to students
- ❏ Without a pass signed by a teacher
- ❏ Inappropriate language to students

Additional explanation: _____

_____

_____

Student signature: _____

Referring teacher: _____

Method of contact (write the phone number or e-mail address): _____

_____

Name of parent/guardian contacted: _____

Date contacted: _____

Time contacted: _____

Result: _____

_____

_____

Resource

Tools for Tiers 2 and 3

BRIEF FUNCTIONAL BEHAVIORAL ASSESSMENT SURVEY/CHECKLIST

Student name: _____   Grade: _____   School: _____

Dates of observation: _____   Completed by: _____

The information below should be completed for a period of five consecutive school days. If the student is absent, the date of absence should be noted and the data collection should continue on the day the student returns to school. The information should be compiled by each of the student's teachers.

Day	Date	Setting	Activity	Description of Behavior	Frequency of Behavior	Time/ Duration	Strategy or Consequence Imposed by Teacher	Response to Strategy or Consequence

ANALYSIS OF DATA

After completing the behavior documentation for a period of time, use the following questions to identify patterns revealed in any area during the data collection period.

Day: Do the problem behaviors occur more often on specific days of the week? ___

If yes, which ones? _____

Setting: Do the problem behaviors occur more often in specific settings or types of settings (e.g., structured vs. unstructured)? Describe. _____

_____

_____

Activity: Do the problem behaviors occur more often during similar types of activities (e.g., when student is asked to read or write)? Describe. _____

_____

_____

Are there any settings where the behavior does not occur? _____

Who is present when the behavior occurs? _____

Setting events: Are there external events or factors that may contribute to the behavior (e.g., conflict in home before school, student isn't feeling well, etc.)? Specify.

_____

_____

Types of behavior: Can the behaviors be categorized into specific categories?

☐ impulsivity ☐ distractibility ☐ withdrawal

☐ aggression toward others ☐ aggression toward self ☐ other _____

Frequency of behavior: How many times does the behavior occur during a time period? _____ times in a _____ minute period

Time/duration: Is there a pattern in the time of day the behavior occurs? How long does the episode last? _____

Strategy or consequence: What types of strategies are most often being implemented with this student? _____

_____

Student response to strategy or consequence: How does the student respond when a consequence is given? _____

References

Achenbach, T. M. (1991). *Integrative guide for the 1991 CBCL/4–18 Yrs., & TRF profiles*. Burlington: University of Vermont, Department of Psychiatry.

Baer, G. G., Manning, M. A., & Shiomi, K. (2006). Children's reasoning about aggressions: Differences between Japan and the United States and implications for school discipline. *School Psychology Review, 35*(1), 62–77.

Barnett, D. W., Elliott, N., Wolsing, L., Bunger, C. E., Haski, H., & McKissick, C., et al. (2006). Response to Intervention for young children with extremely challenging behaviors: What it might look like. *School Psychology Review, 35*(4), 568–582.

Barth, R. (2001). *Learning by heart*. San Francisco: Jossey-Bass.

Bender, W. N., & Shores, C. (2007). *Response to Intervention: A practical guide for every teacher*. Thousand Oaks, CA: Corwin.

Bergan, J. R. (1977). *Behavioral consultation*. Columbus, OH: Charles E. Merrill.

Bloom, B. S. (1984). *Taxonomy of educational objectives: Book 1 cognitive domain*. Reading, MA: Addison-Wesley.

Bryant, D. P., Bryant, B. R., Gersten, R., Scammacca, N., & Chavez, M. M. (2008). Mathematics intervention for first- and second-grade students with mathematics difficulties: The effects of tier 2 intervention delivered as booster lessons. *Remedial and Special Education, 29*(1), 20–32.

Burns, B. J., Schoenwald, S. K., Burchard, J. D., Faw, L., & Santos, A. B. (2000). Comprehensive community-based interventions for youth with severe emotional disorders: Multisystemic therapy and the wraparound process. *Journal of Child and Family Studies, 9*(3), 283–314.

Cancelli, A. S., Harris, A. M., Friedman, D. L., & Yoshida, R. K. (1993). Type of instruction and the relationship of classroom behavior to achievement among learning disabled children. *Journal of Classroom Interaction, 28*(1), 13–21.

Carr, S. C., & Punzo, R. P. (1993). The effects of self-monitoring of academic accuracy and productivity on the performance of students with behavioral disorders. *Behavior Disorders, 18*(4), 241–250.

Carter, D. R., & Horner, R. H. (2007). Adding functional behavioral assessment to First Step to Success: A case study. *Journal of Positive Behavior Interventions, 9*(4), 229–238.

Chafouleas, S., Riley-Tillman, T. C., & Sugai, G. (2007). *School-based behavioral assessment: Informing intervention and instruction*. New York: Guilford Press.

Child Trends Data Bank. (2007). *Teen homicide, suicide, and firearm death*. Retrieved May 26, 2008, from www.childtrendsdatabank.org

Ciechalski, J. C., & Schmidt, M. W. (1995). The effects of social skills training on students with exceptionalities. *Elementary School Guidance and Counseling, 29*(3), 217–222.

Cohen, R., Kincaid, D., & Childs, K. E. (2007). Measuring School-Wide Positive Behavior Support implementation: Development and validation of the Benchmarks of Quality. *Journal of Positive Behavior Interventions, 9*(4), 203–213.

Collaborative for Academic, Social, and Emotional Learning. (2007). *Programs and lessons: Selecting programs.* Retrieved May 15, 2008, from www.casel .org/programs/selecting.php

Colvin, G., & Fernandez, E. (2000). Sustaining effective behavior support systems in an elementary school. *Journal of Positive Behavior Interventions, 2*(4), 251–253.

Conroy, M. A., Sutherland, K. S., Snyder, A. L., & Marsh, S. (2008). Classwide interventions: Effective instruction makes a difference. *TEACHING Exceptional Children, 40*(6), 24–30.

Council for Exceptional Children. (2005). *What's new in the new IDEA 2004?* Arlington, VA: Council for Exceptional Children.

Crimmins, D., Farrell, A. F., Smith, P. W., & Bailey, A. (2007). *Positive strategies for students with behavior problems.* Baltimore: Brookes Publishing.

Crone, D. A., Horner, R. H., & Hawken, L. S. (2004). *Responding to problem behavior in schools.* New York: Guilford Press.

Deno, S., & Mirkin, P. (1977). *Data-based program modification.* Minneapolis, MN: Leadership Training Institute for Special Education.

Dinkes, R., Cataldi, E. F., Kena, G., & Baum, K. (2006). *Indicators of school crime and safety: 2006 (NCES 2007-003/NCJ 214262).* U.S. Departments of Education and Justice. Washington, DC: U.S. Government Printing Office.

Drummond, T. (1994). *The student risk screening scale (SRSS).* Grants Pass, OR: Josephine County Mental Health Program.

DuFour, R., DuFour, R., Eaker, R., & Karhanek, G. (2004). *Whatever it takes: How professional learning communities respond when kids don't learn.* Bloomington, IN: Solution Tree.

Dunlap, G., DePerczel, M., Clarke, S., Wilson, D., Wright, S., & White, R., et al. (1994). Choice making to promote adaptive behavior for students with emotional and behavioral challenges. *Journal of Applied Behavioral Analysis, 27*(3), 505–518.

Dunlap, G., Kern-Dunlap, L., Clarke, S., & Robbins, F. R. (1991). Functional assessment, curricular revision, and sever behavior problems. *Journal of Applied Behavior Analysis, 24*(2), 387–397.

Eber, L., Breen, K., Rose, J., Unizycki, R. M., & London, T. H. (2008). Wraparound as a tertiary level intervention for students with emotional/behavioral needs. *TEACHING Exceptional Children, 40*(6), 16–22.

Eber, L., & Hawken, L. (2008, April). *Sustaining and scaling the implementation of PBIS: Secondary tier and tertiary tier interventions and systems.* Presentation at the National Council for Exceptional Children's Conference, Boston.

Eber, L., Sugai, G., Smith, C. R., & Scott, T. M. (2002). Wraparound and positive behavioral interventions and supports in the schools. *Journal of Emotional and Behavioral Disorders, 10*(3), 171–180.

Ellingson, S. A., Miltenberger, R. G., Stricker, J., Galensky, T. L., & Garlinghouse, M. (2000). Functional assessment and intervention for challenging behaviors in the classroom by general classroom teachers. *Journal of Positive Behavior Interventions, 2*(2), 85–97.

Epstein, M., & Walker, H. (2002). Special education: Best practices and First Step to Success. In B. Burns & K. Hoagwood (Eds.), *Community treatment for youth: Evidence-based intervention for severe emotional and behavioral disorders* (pp. 177–197). New York: Oxford University Press.

Fairbanks, S., Simonsen, B., & Sugai, G. (2008). Classwide secondary and tertiary tier practices and supports. *TEACHING Exceptional Children, 40*(6), 44–52.

Fairbanks, S., Sugai, G., Guardino, D., & Lathrop, M. (2007). Response to Intervention: Examining classroom behavior support in second grade. *Exceptional Children, 73*(3), 288–310.

Forum on Child and Family Statistics. (2007). *American's children: Key national indicators of well-being*. Retrieved May 26, 2008, from www.childstats.gov

Fuchs, D., & Fuchs, L. S. (2005). Responsiveness-to-intervention: A blueprint for practitioners, policymakers, and parents. *TEACHING Exceptional Children, 38*(1), 57–61.

Fuchs, D., Mock, D., Morgan, P. L., & Young, C. L. (2003). Responsiveness-to-intervention: Definitions, evidence, and implications for the learning disabilities construct. *Learning Disabilities Research and Practice, 18*(3), 157–171.

Fuchs, L. S., & Fuchs, D. (2001). Principles for sustaining research-based practice in the schools: A case study. *Focus on Exceptional Children, 33*(6), 1–14.

Fuchs, L. S., & Fuchs, D. (2007). A model for implementing responsiveness to intervention. *TEACHING Exceptional Children, 39*(5), 14–20.

Fuchs, L. S., Fuchs, D., Hamlett, C. L., Hope, S. K., Hollenbeck, K. N., & Capizzi, A. M., et al. (2006). Extending responsiveness-to-intervention to math problem-solving at third grade. *TEACHING Exceptional Children, 38*(4), 59–63.

George, H. P., & Kincaid, D. K. (2008). Building district-level capacity for positive behavior support. *Journal of Positive Behavior Interventions, 10*(1), 20–32.

Georgia Department of Education. (2008). *Georgia performance standards*. Retrieved September 24, 2008, from www.doe.k12.ga.us

Goodman, R. (1997). The Strengths and Difficulties Questionnaire: A research note. *Journal of Child Psychology and Psychiatry, and Allied Disciplines, 38*(5), 581–586.

Gorton, R., Alston, J. A., & Snowden, P. (2007). *School leadership and administration: Important concepts, case studies, and simulations* (7th ed.). New York: McGraw-Hill.

Greenwood, C. R., Kamps, D., Terry, B. J., & Linebarger, D. L. (2007). Primary intervention: A means of preventing special education? In D. Haager, J. Klingner, & S. Vaughn (Eds.), *Evidence-based reading practices for Response to Intervention* (pp. 73–103). Baltimore: Brookes Publishing.

Gresham, F. M. (2003). Establishing the technical adequacy of functional behavioral assessment: Conceptual and measurement challenges. *Behavior Disorders, 28*(3), 282–298.

Harlacher, J. E., Roberts, N. E., & Merrell, K. W. (2006). Classwide interventions for students with ADHD: A summary of teacher options beneficial for the whole class. *TEACHING Exceptional Children, 39*(2), 6–12.

Hawken, L. S., & Horner, R. H. (2003). Implementing a targeted group intervention within a school-wide system of behavior support. *Journal of Behavioral Education, 12*(3), 225–240.

Heacox, D. (2002). *Differentiating instruction in the regular classroom*. Minneapolis, MN: Free Spirit.

Hilton, A. (2007). Response to Intervention: Changing how we do business. *Leadership, 36*(4), 16–19.

Hoffman, A., & Field, S. (2005). *Steps to self-determination: A curriculum to help adolescents learn to achieve their goals.* Austin, TX: Pro-Ed.

Horner, R., Hawken, L., & March, R. (2008, March 26). *Targeted interventions.* Retrieved April 30, 2008, from www.pbis.org

Horner, R., Salantine, S., & Albin, R. (2003). *Self assessment of contextual fit in schools.* Eugene: University of Oregon, Educational and Community Supports.

Horner, R., & Sugai, G. (2007a, February 6). *Linking behavior support and literacy support.* Retrieved May 5, 2008, from www.pbis.org/pastconferencepresentations.htm

Horner, R., & Sugai, G. (2007b, February 6). *School-wide Positive Behavior Support.* Retrieved May 5, 2008, from www.pbis.org/pastconferencepresentations.htm

Horner, R. H., & Sugai, G. (2000). School-wide behavior support: An emerging initiative. *Journal of Positive Behavior Interventions, 2*(4), 231–232.

Horner, R. H., Sugai, G., Todd, A. W., & Lewis-Palmer, T. (2005). *Individualized supports for students with problem behaviors: Designing positive behavior plans.* New York: Guilford Press.

Hosp, M. K., Hosp, J. L., & Howell, K. W. (2007). *The ABCs of CBM: A practical guide to curriculum-based measurement.* New York: Guilford Press.

Individuals with Disabilities Education Improvement Act of 2004, Federal Register 71 §614(b)(6) (2004).

Ingram, K., Lewis-Palmer, T., & Sugai, G. (2005). Function-based intervention planning: Comparing the effectiveness of FBA function-based and non-function-based intervention plans. *Journal of Positive Behavior Interventions, 7*(4), 224–237.

Irvin, L. K., Tobin, T. J., Sprague, J. R., Sugai, G., & Vincent, C. G. (2004). Validity of office discipline referral measures as indices of school-wide behavioral status and effects of school-wide behavioral interventions. *Journal of Positive Behavior Interventions, 6*(3), 131–147.

Janney, R., & Snell, M. E. (2008). *Behavioral support.* Baltimore: Brookes Publishing.

Johnson, P. (2001). Dimensions of functioning in alcoholic and nonalcoholic families. *Journal of Mental Health, 23*(2), 127–136.

Kamps, D., Abbott, M., Greenwood, C., Wills, H., Veerkamp, M., & Kaufman, J. (2008). Effects of small-group reading instruction and curriculum differences for students most at risk in kindergarten: Two-year results for secondary- and tertiary-level interventions. *Journal of Learning Disabilities, 41*(1), 101–114.

Kennedy, C. H. (2000). When reinforcers for problem behavior are not readily apparent: Extending functional assessments to complex problem behaviors. *Journal of Positive Behavior Interventions, 2*(4), 195–201.

Kern, L., & Manz, P. (2004). A look at current validity issues of school-wide behavior support. *Behavioral Disorders, 30*(1), 47–59.

Kern, L., Vorndran, C. M., Hilt, A., Ringdahl, J. E., Adelman, B. E., & Dunlap, G. (1998). Choice as an intervention to improve behavior: A review of the literature. *Journal of Behavioral Education, 8*(2), 151–169.

Killu, K., Weber, K. P., Derby, K. M., & Barretto, A. (2006). Behavior intervention planning and implementation of positive behavioral support plans: An examination of states' adherence to standards for practice. *Journal of Positive Behavior Interventions, 8*(4), 195–200.

Kincaid, D., Childs, K., Blase, K. A., & Wallace, F. (2007). Identifying barriers and facilitators in implementing schoolwide Positive Behavior Support. *Journal of Positive Behavior Interventions, 9*(3), 174–184.

Klingner, J. K., Arguelles, M. E., Hughes, M. T., & Vaughn, S. (2001). Examining the schoolwide "spread" of research-based practices. *Learning Disability Quarterly, 24*(4), 221–234.

Kovaleski, J. K. (2007). Response to Intervention: Considerations for research and systems change. *School Psychology Review, 36*(4), 638–646.

Kratochwill, T. R., Volpiansky, P., Clements, M., & Ball, C. (2007). Professional development in implementing and sustaining multitier prevention models: Implications for Response to Intervention. *School Psychology Review, 36*(4), 618–631.

Lane, K. L., Parks, R. J., Kalberg, J. R., & Carter, E. W. (2007). Systematic screening at the middle school level: Score reliability and validity of the student risk screening scale. *Journal of Emotional and Behavioral Disorders, 15*(4), 209–222.

Lane, K. L., Wehby, J. H., Robertson, E. J., & Rogers, L. A. (2007). How do different types of high school students respond to School-Wide Positive Behavior Support programs? Characteristics and responsiveness of teacher-identified students. *Journal of Emotional and Behavioral Disorders, 15*(1), 3–20.

Lavoie, R. (2007). *The motivation breakthrough: Six secrets to turning on the tuned-out child.* New York: Touchstone.

Lien-Thorne, S., & Kamps, D. (2005). Replication study of the First Step to Success early intervention program. *Behavioral Disorders, 31*, 18–32.

Lohrmann-O'Rourke, S., Knoster, T., Sabatine, K., Smith, D., Horvath, B., & Llewellyn, G. (2000). School-wide application of PBS in the Bangor Area School District. *Journal of Positive Behavior Interventions, 2*(4), 238–240.

March, R., Horner, R. H., Lewis-Palmer, T., Brown, D., Crone, D., & Todd, A. W., et al. (2000). *Functional assessment checklist for teachers and staff (FACTS).* Eugene: University of Oregon, Department of Educational and Community Supports.

Martin, J., & Marshall, L. H. (1996). ChoiceMaker: Infusing self-determination instruction into the IEP and transition process. In D. Sands & M. Wehmeyer (Eds.), *Self-determination across the lifespan* (pp. 215–236). Baltimore: Brookes Publishing.

Marzano, R. J., Marzano, J. S., & Pickering, D. J. (2003). *Classroom management that works: Research-based strategies for every teacher.* Alexandria, VA: Association for Supervision and Curriculum Development.

Mass-Galloway, R. L., Panyan, M. V., Smith, C. R., & Wessendorf, S. (2008). Systems change with School-Wide Positive Behavior Supports. *Journal of Positive Behavior Interventions, 10*(2), 129–135.

Mather, N., & Goldstein, S. (2008). *Learning disabilities and challenging behaviors: A guide to intervention and classroom management* (2nd ed.). Baltimore: Brookes Publishing.

McIntosh, K., Borgmeier, C., Anderson, C. M., Horner, R. H., Rodriguez, B. J., & Tobin, T. J. (2008). Technical adequacy of the Functional Assessment Checklist: Teachers and Staff (FACTS) FBA Interview Measure. *Journal of Positive Behavior Interventions, 10*(1), 33–45.

McIntosh, K., Chard, D. J., Boland, J. B., & Horner, R. H. (2006). Demonstration of combined efforts in school-wide academic and behavioral systems and incidence of reading and behavior challenges in early elementary grades. *Journal of Positive Behavior Interventions, 8*(3), 146–154.

McQuillian, K., & DuPaul, G. J. (1996). Classroom performance of students with serious emotional disturbance: A comparative study of evaluation methods for behavior management. *Journal of Emotional and Behavioral Disorders, 4*(3), 162–170.

Mellard, D. F., & Johnson, E. (2008). *RTI: A practitioner's guide to implementing Response to Intervention.* Thousand Oaks, CA: Corwin.

Meyers, A., & Eisenman, L. (2005). Student-led IEPs: Take the first step. *TEACHING Exceptional Children, 37*(4), 52–58.

Michaelis, V. (2008, August 15). Can Phelps ever be topped? *USA Today,* pp. 1–2A.

Miranda, L. C. (1991). *Latino child poverty in the United States.* Washington, DC: Children's Defense Fund.

Nakasato, J. (2000). Data-based decision making in Hawaii's behavior support effort. *Journal of Positive Behavior Interventions, 2*(4), 247–251.

National Data Analysis System. (2007). *Child abuse and neglect.* Retrieved May 26, 2008, from http://ndas.cwla.org

National Education Goals Panel. (2000). *National education goals.* Retrieved May 4, 2008, from http://govinfo.library.unt.edu/negp

National Mathematics Advisory Panel. (2008, March). *Foundations for success: National Mathematics Advisory Panel final report.* Retrieved May 15, 2008, from www.ed.gov/about/bdscomm/mathpanel

National Reading Panel. (2007). *Put reading first: The research building blocks for teaching children to read.* Retrieved August 15, 2007, from www.national readingpanel.org

National Staff Development Council. (2001). NSDC's standards for staff development. Retrieved July 24, 2007, from www.nsdc.org/standards/index.cfm

National Technical Assistance Center on Positive Behavioral Interventions and Supports. (2007). *What is school-wide PBS?* Retrieved September 2, 2007, from www.pbis.org

Nersesian, M., Todd, A. W., Lehmann, J., & Watson, J. (2000). School-wide behavior support through district-level system change. *Journal of Positive Behavior Interventions, 2*(4), 244–247.

No Child Left Behind Act. (2001). Section 9101[37]. Retrieved March 12, 2008, from www.ed.gov/policy/elsec/leg/esea02/index.html

O'Neill, R. E., Horner, R. H., Ablin, R. W., Sprague, J. R., Storey, K., & Newton, J. S. (1997). *Functional assessment and program development for problem behaviors: A practical handbook.* New York: Brooks/Cole.

OSEP Center on Positive Behavioral Interventions and Supports. (2004). *School-wide positive behavior support implementers' blueprint and self-assessment.* Retrieved May 12, 2008, from www.osepideasthatwork.org/toolkit/pdf/SchoolwideBehaviorSupport.pdf

Patton, B., Jolivette, K., & Ramsey, M. (2006). Students with emotional and behavioral disorders can manage their own behavior. *TEACHING Exceptional Children, 39*(2), 14–21.

Payne, R. K. (2005). *A framework for understanding poverty* (4th ed.). Highlands, TX: aha! Process.

President's Commission on Excellence in Special Education. (2002). *A new era: Revitalizing special education for children and their families.* Retrieved July 26, 2006, from www.ed.gov/inits/commissionsboards/index.html

Rainbows International. (2008). *Rainbows programs.* Retrieved May 26, 2008, from www.rainbows.org

Reid, R., & Lienemann, T. O. (2006). Self-regulated strategy development for written expression with students with Attention-Deficit/Hyperactivity Disorder. *Exceptional Children, 73*(1), 53–68.

Reid, R., Trout, A. L., & Schartz, M. (2005). Self-regulation interventions for children with Attention-Deficit/Hyperactivity Disorder. *Exceptional Children, 71*(4), 361–377.

Rief, S. F. (2005). *How to reach and teach children with ADD/ADHD* (2nd ed.). San Francisco: Jossey-Bass.

Rock, M. L. (2005). Use of strategic self-monitoring to enhance academic engagement, productivity, and accuracy of students with and without exceptionalities. *Journal of Positive Behavior Interventions, 7*(1), 3–17.

Sadler, C. (2000). Effective behavior support implementation at the district level: Tigard-Tualatin School District. *Journal of Positive Behavior Interventions, 2*(4), 241–243.

Sandomierski, T., Kincaid, D., & Algozinne, B. (2007). Response to Intervention and Positive Behavior Support: Brothers from different mothers or sisters from different misters? *Positive Behavioral Interventions and Supports Newsletter, 4*(2), 1–5.

School-Wide Information System. (2008). *What is SWIS?* Retrieved May 8, 2008, from www.swis.org

Scott, T. M. (2001). A schoolwide example of positive behavioral supports. *Journal of Positive Behavior Interventions, 3*(2), 88–94.

Seybert, S., Dunlap, G., & Ferro, J. (1996). The effects of choice-making on the problem behaviors of high school students with intellectual disabilities. *Journal of Behavioral Education, 6*(1), 49–65.

Shores, C. F., & Chester, K. (2008). *Using RTI for school improvement: Raising the achievement of all students.* Thousand Oaks, CA: Corwin.

Simmons, D. C., Coyne, M. D., Kwok, O., McDonagh, S., Harn, B. A., & Kame'enui, E. J. (2008). Indexing Response to Intervention: A longitudinal study of reading risk from kindergarten through third grade. *Journal of Learning Disabilities, 4*(2), 158–173.

Simonsen, B., Sugai, G., & Negron, M. (2008). School positive behavior supports: Primary systems and practices. *TEACHING Exceptional Children, 40*(6), 32–40.

Sindelar, P., Shearer, D., Yendol-Hoppey, D., & Liebert, T. (2006). The sustainability of inclusive school reform. *Exceptional Children, 72*(3), 317–331.

Sprague, J., Walker, H., Stiebler, S., Simonsen, B., Nishioka, V., & Wagner, L. (2001). Exploring the relationship between school discipline referrals and delinquency. *Psychology in the Schools, 38*(2), 197–206.

Sprick, R., Garrison, M., & Howard, L. M. (1998). *CHAMPs: A proactive and positive approach to classroom management.* Longmont, CO: Sopris West.

Sprick, R. S. (2006). *Discipline in the Secondary Classroom* (2nd ed.). San Francisco: Jossey-Bass.

Stahr, B., Cushing, D., Lane, K., & Fox, J. (2006). Efficacy of a function-based intervention in decreasing off-task behavior exhibited by a student with ADHD. *Journal of Positive Behavior Interventions, 8*(4), 201–211.

Stecker, P. M. (2006). *Monitoring student progress in individualized educational programs using curriculum-based measurement.* Retrieved September 15, 2007, from www.studentprogress.org

Stewart, R. M., Benner, G. J., Martella, R. C., & Marchand-Martella, N. E. (2007). Three-tier models of reading and behavior: A research review. *Journal of Positive Behavior Interventions, 9*(4), 239–253.

Sugai, G. (2008). *School-wide Positive Behavior Support and Response to Intervention.* Retrieved September 5, 2008, from www.rtinetwork.org

Sugai, G., & Horner, R. H. (2002). The evolution of discipline practices: Schoolwide positive behavior supports. *Behavior Psychology in the Schools, 24*(1), 23–50.

Sugai, G., Horner, R. H., Dunlap, G., Heineman, M., Lewis, T. J., & Nelson, C. M., et al. (2000). Applying positive behavioral support and functional assessment in schools. *Journal of Positive Behavior Interventions, 2*(3), 131–143.

Sugai, G., Horner, R. H., & Gresham, F. M. (2002). *Interventions for academic and behavior problems II: Preventative and remedial approaches.* Bethesda, MD: National Association of School Psychologists.

Sugai, G., Sprague, J., Horner, R., & Walker, H. (2000). Preventing school violence: The use of office referral to assess and monitor school-wide discipline interventions. *Journal of Emotional and Behavioral Disorders, 8*(2), 94–101.

Taylor-Greene, S. J., & Kartub, D. T. (2000). Durable implementation of schoolwide behavior support: The high five program. *Journal of Positive Behavior Interventions, 2*(4), 233–235.

Tobin, T. J., & Sugai, G. (1999). Using sixth-grade school records to predict violence, chronic discipline problems, and high school outcomes. *Journal of Emotional and Behavioral Disorders, 7*(1), 40–53.

Todd, A. W., Campbell, A. L., Meyer, G. G., & Horner, R. H. (2008). The effects of a targeted intervention to reduce problem behaviors: Elementary school implementation of check in-check out. *Journal of Positive Behavior Interventions, 10*(1), 46–55.

Tomlinson, C. A. (1999). *The differentiated classroom: Responding to the needs of all learners.* Alexandria, VA: Association for Supervision and Curriculum Development.

Turnbull, A., Edmonson, H., Griggs, P., Wickham, D., Sailor, W., & Freeman, R., et al. (2002). A blueprint for schoolwide positive behavior support: Implementation of three components. *Exceptional Children, 68*(3), 377–402.

U.S. Office of Education. (1999). *Assistance to states for the education of children with disabilities: Final rule.* Federal Register 34 CFR Part 300, sec 300.520.

Vaughn, S., Linan-Thompson, S., Mathes, P. G., Cirino, P. T., Carlson, C. D., & Pollard-Durodola, S. D., et al. (2006). Effectiveness of Spanish intervention for first-grade English language learners at risk for reading difficulties. *Journal of Learning Disabilities, 39*(1), 56–73.

Vaughn, S., & Roberts, G. (2007). Secondary interventions in reading: Providing additional instruction for students at risk. *TEACHING Exceptional Children, 39*(5), 40–46.

Vellutino, F. R., Scanlon, D. M., Small, S., & Fanuele, D. P. (2006). Response to intervention as a vehicle for distinguishing between children with and without reading disabilities: Evidence for the role of kindergarten and first grade interventions. *Journal of Learning Disabilities, 39*(2), 157–169.

Von Ravensberg, H., & Tobin, T. J. (2006). *IDEA 2004 final regulations: The reauthorized functional behavioral assessment.* Retrieved April 23, 2008, from www.pbis.org

Waguespack, A., Vaccaro, T., & Continere, L. (2006). Functional behavioral assessment and intervention with emotional/behaviorally disordered students: In pursuit of state of the art. *International Journal of Behavioral Consultation and Therapy, 2*(4), 463–473.

Walker, B., Cheney, D., Stage, S., & Blum, C. (2005). Schoolwide screening and positive behavior supports: Identifying and supporting students at risk for school failure. *Journal of Positive Behavior Interventions, 7*(4), 194–204.

Walker, H., Colvin, G., & Ramsey, E. (1995). *Antisocial behavior in schools: Strategies and best practices.* Baltimore: Brookes Publishing.

Walker, H., & Severson, H. H. (1992). *Systematic screening for behavior disorders.* Longmont, CO: Sopris West.

Wehmeyer, M. L., Baker, D. J., Blumberg, R., & Harrison, R. (2004). Self-determination and student involvement in functional assessment: Innovative practices. *Journal of Positive Behavior Interventions, 6*(1), 29–35.

Wiggins, G., & McTighe, J. (2005). *Understanding by design* (2nd ed.). Alexandria, VA: Association for Supervision and Curriculum Development.

Winerip, M. (2008, August 10). Phelps's mother recalls helping her son find gold-medal focus. *The New York Times*, p. 4.

Witt, J. C., & Elliott, S. N. (1985). Acceptability of classroom intervention strategies. In T. R. Kratochwill (Ed.), *Advances in school psychology, IV*, 251–288. Hillsdale, NJ: Erlbaum.

Wright-Gallo, G., Higbee, T., Reagon, K., & Davey, B. (2006). Classroom-based functional analysis and intervention for students with emotional/behavioral disorders. *Education and Treatment of Children, 29*(3), 421–435.

Yeaton, W. H., & Sechrest, L. (1981). Critical dimensions in the choice and maintenance of successful treatments: Strength, integrity, and effectiveness. *Journal of Consulting and Clinical Psychology, 49*(2), 156–167.

Zirkel, P. A., & Krohn, N. (2008). RTI after IDEA: A survey of state laws. *TEACHING Exceptional Children, 40*(3), 71–73.

Index

CORWIN
A SAGE Company

The Corwin logo—a raven striding across an open book—represents the union of courage and learning. Corwin is committed to improving education for all learners by publishing books and other professional development resources for those serving the field of PreK–12 education. By providing practical, hands-on materials, Corwin continues to carry out the promise of its motto: **"Helping Educators Do Their Work Better."**